Beyond Selling:
Realizing Value, Boosting Results

By: Dr. Amir Kahani

Discover the Keys to Unrivaled Sales Achievement

Copyright ©2024 *Dr. Amir Kahani*

All rights reserved.

Table Of Contents

Dedication 6
About the Author 7
Introduction 9
CHAPTER 1: NEUROPSYCOANALYSIS 19
   Buying Process as an Engine for Business 23
CHAPTER 2: DEFINING A TARGET AUDIENCE 26
   What Emotion Motivates the Target Audience To Purchase? 27
   The Gap Between The Market And The Existing Solutions 27
   The Difference between the Price Of Existing Solutions And The Financial Value Of Your Solution 28
   The Value of Your Solution to The Value Of The Best Product Competing With You. 29
   How far does the concept of shared value creation extend? 32
CHAPTER 3: CUSTOMERS 34
Finding your end Customers 34
   What Will Make The End-Customer Buy From My Customers? 35
CHAPTER 4: CRAFTING A STRATEGIC PLAN 43
UBC, Branding, and Market Positioning 43
   What is the Difference between the Direct Customer and the End Customer? 44
   What is Market Positioning? 47

- Leveraging UBC and Branding for Effective Market Positioning 47
- Importance of understanding customer awareness 49

CHAPTER 5: MANAGING AND HARNESSING STAKEHOLDERS 52

A Continuous Action Plan 52
- Understanding Stakeholder Management 52
- Benefits of Effective Stakeholder Management 52
- Key principles and approaches to stakeholder management 53
- Identifying and Prioritizing Stakeholders 54
- What is Market Positioning? 54

CHAPTER 6: BUILDING STRATEGY 60

Building the Short-Term Startup Strategy under Conditions of Uncertainty 60
- Should you develop additional products or expand to new target audiences with the existing products? 60
- Should you enter new sectors or provide a broader response to existing customers? 61
- When is it right to enter into a merger or strategic collaboration? 62
- How to upgrade the product, overcome the competitors, and reach a larger market share? 63
- Dynamic and Changing Business Strategy 68

CHAPTER 7: RESULTS-ORIENTED MANAGEMENT 69
- Netflix - Leveraging Results-Oriented Management for Innovation and Growth 82
- Leveraging ROWE for Innovation 83
- Adobe - Empowering Innovation and Creativity through Results-Oriented Management 84

Adobe's ROWE philosophy revolves around several key principles 85

CHAPTER 8: BUILDING STRONG FOUNDATIONS BEFORE HIRING 89

What do I or we want our legacy in the tech world to be? 90

The Role of Values in Decision-Making and Company Identity 91

Harmonizing the Heartbeats: Merging Personal Beliefs with Corporate Ethos 92

Structuring Better Teams: Elevating the Hiring Journey with Feedback Magic 93

Charting the Fluid Blueprint: Embracing Evolution in Tech Teams 99

CHAPTER 9: LEADERSHIP IN THE DIGITAL AGE 103

The Impact of Manager Presence: Beyond Physical Proximity 103

CHAPTER 10: BUSINESS PROCESS MANAGEMENT 118

CHAPTER 11: AUGMENTING SALES 128

How AI, VR, and Future Tech Are Revolutionizing the Game 128

CONCLUSION 149

A Vision for Harmonious Prosperity 149

Dedication

I would like to dedicate this book to my family.

About the Author

Dr. Amir Kahani implements the robust VSO methodology, his exclusive method, which keeps integrity intact and helps companies grow in challenging conditions. This model is a crucial component of your business strategy since it guarantees that your business endeavor will increase revenue, enhance brand excellence, and create enduring trust in the industry.

With a PhD in Economics from Varna Free University and an MBA from the University of Manchester, Dr. Amir Kahani has the analytical skills and economic understanding needed to develop business growth strategies that don't compromise ethical values. This promise will comfort your audience and give them faith in your business.

Website: www.amirkahani.com

LinkedIn: https://www.linkedin.com/in/amir-kahani/

Building Business from the Ground Up the Value Chain

Introduction

"The business changes. The technology changes. The team members change. The problem isn't change, per se, because change is going to happen anyway; the problem, rather, is the inability to cope with change when it comes."
— Kent Beck.

Many businesses take a myopic approach to profit-making. For a layman, the core business objective may be profit-maximizing, but that shouldn't be the case for a good entrepreneur. I mean, it has been this way for eons now, but the business landscape has changed drastically, and there have been many developments in how businesses operate.

Ever since the technological shift, many startups and entrepreneurial activities have explored new ways of running a business. This is what I love about business dynamism: good and smart businesses learn, innovate, and streamline. Ordinary businesses do not learn or change anything. They stick to a conventional pathway, eventually exhausting resources, finances, and, ultimately, the motivation to run a business.

In the modern world, which is very data-driven, businesses jump onto any opportunity that comes their way. There was a time when Nokia would build a product and then sleep on it, letting competition disrupt the industry by building consumer-oriented products and capturing market share overnight.

Still, there are companies out there struggling to understand what business dynamism really is and how the old practices are changing as we make progress in technology. Globalization is a cherry on top for businesses that want to explore beyond geographical boundaries, but it is truly an art to tap a market you know very little about.

Let's be fair—you must stay vigilant and watch your competitors' actions to stay updated. In a world where data related to consumer preferences is easily available, if your business still fails to attract the right customers and your answer to whether your business growth is declining despite all your efforts to sustain it is "yes," then you're NOT doing it right!

Nokia was once one of the leading cell phone manufacturers in the world. However, it failed to embrace the shift towards smartphones and stuck with its existing product lines, which ultimately caused its market share to drop drastically over time.

It is a classic example of what myopia does to a business. Sure, their product lines were making money and turning a profit, but they completely missed out on the shift towards smartphones, which was transforming the mobile phone industry.

In hindsight, it is clear that Nokia should have been more agile in adapting to new technology and consumer demands. If they had embraced the smartphone revolution earlier, they could have stayed ahead of their competitors instead of languishing behind them in market share. This is an important lesson for businesses today - you must be willing to adapt and innovate, or you risk becoming irrelevant.

No matter what kind of business you operate, staying on top of trends and anticipating customer needs is essential if you want to remain competitive in your market. Your business's success depends on it! Nokia's decline is a cautionary tale for businesses everywhere—staying innovative and responsive to customer needs is essential if you want to remain competitive.

On the other hand, we have Apple, who embraced the shift to smartphones and created one of the most popular mobile phones in history—the iPhone. Apple's success is a testament to its ability to innovate and stay ahead of market trends. They have shown us that being agile and responsive to consumer needs pays off. The lesson here is clear: if you want your business to succeed, you must stay abreast of new technologies, customer demands, and industry trends.

For years, I have been observing businesses and witnessing their rise and fall. My name is Amir Kahani, and I am an entrepreneur with over thirty years of experience in sales. ; I can vouch for the fact that for businesses to take an inside-out approach, paired with a myopic vision, is a path to failure in this era of a dynamic business environment. From the beginning, I was passionate about the business environment and the factors that could greatly impact its growth. I earned a bachelor's degree in economics and political science from Bar-Ilan University, Israel, and then I moved to England to pursue an MBA from the University of Manchester. I earned my Ph.D. in Economics, specializing in value-based pricing.

This is where I started looking at businesses from a more practical lens. I got a role at a leading International consulting firm, where I now work as a managing partner to lead a team of professional business consultants. It was no doubt a challenging career path, and it required me to stay updated on the new developments occurring in the business sector and monitor the political and economic situation of countries. As for the consultants working under me, they would assist businesses in maintaining growth levels and would oversee all required business aspects such as business development, marketing and sales, finance, taxation, audit, and so forth.

While associated with my company, I am also an international public speaker, writer, and lecturer at Netanya Academic College. Since I've been in the consulting industry, I do best talking to people and advising them on matters. I aim to improve society's ecosystem by improving the value that people give to society. I am also certified in martial arts and Zen Shiatsu, and I have incorporated the martial arts and Zen Shiatsu principles into my personal and professional life.

My years of practicing in the consulting industry helped me highlight a single problem persisting throughout all businesses—taking an inward approach, i.e., focusing more on company resources rather than on what the consumers want. I saw many businesses fail, and I noticed a pattern in all of them.

When sellers develop a business plan, they determine their target audience, develop a product or a service to offer, and determine its pricing, the supply chain process, and marketing channels. It's all the same; every business takes the same route repeatedly. Their entire business models are focused on selling; they only look at two things while devising their models – value proposition and profit maximization. This is the oldest way of conducting business. Their main priority is to make a profit, and they want to look at the business' revenue stream before anything else, which is a very narrow approach.

You can even read up on expert advice, and they all have the same thing to say about the effective methods of doubling or tripling your sales, value selling, and other business aspects. Every business department solely focuses on selling without realizing that this approach can damage the company in the long run.

This approach is the reason that hundreds of businesses fail every year. And I've witnessed that first-hand.

Giants like Nokia may or may not survive their short-sightedness, but if you're a Small and Mid-size Enterprise (, making this mistake can instantly get you out of business.

So, what keeps you in the business?

In simple words, the second element of the business model is the customer value proposition.

You can't build a product and expect people to buy it unless it's innovative, such as Apple products, which can easily take the global markets by storm. Even their products are made after a lot of market research, and their value propositions are actually what we want as customers. We all embraced AirPods as soon as they dropped. Before Apple launched them, we didn't know we even needed them.

But this doesn't occur often.

'What if no one wants to buy your product? Will you still be able to generate any profit? Of course not. Hence, it is evident that the important aspect of your business is not selling but the buying intention of your prospects. Your businesses cannot become successful just because you want to sell your products or services. Instead, the secret behind a business's success is that someone wants to buy your products or services. If your clothes don't fit all sizes, your prospects won't buy them. If your prices are too high, no one will be interested in buying them. Therefore, understanding the needs and wants of your prospects is critical for success. Otherwise, you'll end up losing money.'''

This doesn't just hold for B2C companies but is also relevant to B2B companies.

Suppose you're a car manufacturer with multiple dealers in different cities to whom you distribute your cars. However, these dealers will only buy from you if their customers demand it. Otherwise, they will stop doing business with you.

The lesson?

Your clients' clients, or as it is called the end-consumer, are equally important to you as they are your clients, too. And to run your business successfully, you will need to think from your end-consumer perspective and come up with products that are widely demanded. Years ago, when Costco started operating, they would only keep specific categories and SKUs that they knew would actually sell out in their warehouses to keep the costs at a minimum. It focused on its clients' and end-customers' needs, and that's how it managed to survive in a marketplace where there are many giants like Walmart.

As an entrepreneur or business owner, firms need to think beyond simply providing a commodity to customers. Successful business owners should always have their customers in mind and the needs that their products will fulfill. It is not enough for entrepreneurs to make a short-term stab at creating something with immediate monetary reward. Instead, business owners should create something authentically engaging with customers' needs to encourage loyalty and long-term success. Streamlining this Process starts by identifying and understanding the end customer; how can a product be packaged appropriately and presented if its intended customer hasn't been considered? With research into end-customer specifications a priority, entrepreneurs can focus on innovative solutions and designs that meet the customer's needs from beginning to end.

In the contemporary business environment, marketing and sales are no longer considered as isolated silos with distinct roles. Instead, they are tightly interconnected, forming an integral part of a unified strategy for organizational success. Their relationship is particularly prominent during the customer's journey, a path marked by continuous search for information, decision-making, and eventual purchasing.

In this digital age, customers often embark on a research journey before purchasing, delving into a sea of online information about the organization and its offerings. It's important to remember that potential clients may have inherent fears or apprehensions during this buying process. Therefore, the organization's responsibility is to dissipate these concerns by strategically "pushing" relevant and reassuring content online, reinforcing the prospective customer's trust.

In this context, marketing plays a crucial role in creating a positive image and awareness of the company among its target customers. It involves developing engaging advertisements and campaigns designed to ignite interest and convey a sense of reliability about the products or services. Meanwhile, sales build upon this foundation of interest and trust, transforming it into concrete deals.

Beyond this, both marketing and sales are also involved in post-purchase engagement. This could include following up with existing clients to ensure they are utilizing the products or services correctly, addressing their queries, and sustaining their satisfaction levels.

The buying process is a journey that customers take to bridge the gap between their current situation and the future they desire. Customers must decide what product they need and assess if it meets their needs. They have to understand their needs, which often requires research and understanding of the market. After discovering whether the product checks all their boxes, customers decide how this purchase will help them get from an unsatisfactory situation into one that better meets their expectations for the future. Thus, customer decisions reflect their here-and-now concerns and hope for what lies ahead.

This process is an integral part of running any successful business, directing activities, and helping identify target audiences to achieve maximum results. It starts with a customer looking for a solution who, in the case of larger organizations, can involve many different stakeholders, such as the finance department or IT department. For example, when deciding to purchase software, it's not always the IT department that is the end user but instead a higher-level individual such as a financial executive whose wants and needs must be considered. Ultimately, it's essential to understand all aspects of the buying process – both from the perspective of those making purchases and those receiving them – to ensure businesses achieve their goals effectively.

Moreover, fear can be a significant motivator when it comes to finding solutions, and it's especially true when dealing with different customers. Everyone has a unique emotional channel that drives them to act to prevent a negative or unwanted outcome. Take the example of the financial analyst in the finance department whose fear is likely caused by an overwhelming amount of data and the fear that they won't be able to provide accurate forecasts as a result. Acting on this fear could prompt them to devise solutions proactively and efficiently, knowing that the worst possible outcome could happen if no action were taken. It is also important to consider that different types of fears are connected to various types of people – it's all about understanding what drives each individual and being aware of what kind of motivation works best for each person.

As a salesperson, one of the most important factors to keep in mind is the needs and fears of your customers. It's up to you to figure out what reasons or potential risks customers may have when considering your product. Once identified, addressing those concerns is crucial so they feel comfortable moving forward with the purchase. Doing so makes it easier for customers to make an informed decision without worrying too much. This kind of relationship allows them to trust in what you're selling while knowing that their questions were answered honestly and without bias. In the end, understanding your end customer's fears isn't just beneficial for making a sale - it can help build relationships and establish trust in your brand for years to come.

Rather than simply pushing products at customers, I want organizations to seek and create an environment where the business can truly understand what their customers seek. This requires an in-depth analysis of what they are offering compared to what others are providing - a strategy designed to generate a triple-win scenario for everyone involved. By doing so, they open up avenues previously undiscovered, enhance customer satisfaction, and streamline their own approach to sales and marketing. Ultimately, these three-pronged benefits create opportunities for both businesses and customers alike. The needed turn can cause a massive change – a much-needed one in the business landscape, transforming how entrepreneurs view sales, marketing, and R&D.

Consequently, this means the key to success in modern business is understanding the customer's buying process, not only for the initial sale but for their overall experience. This requires planning and strategy since it doesn't happen overnight. Businesses need to focus on their customers' needs, focusing not just on short-term sales but also on how to continue to strengthen and improve the customer-business relationship over time. Flexibility and agility are required to create an environment that constantly grows and evolves with its customers. Every action must be taken with consideration of your customer in mind--it's all about finding a balance between catering to their needs and giving them unique experiences. I communicate this to my clients and students looking to succeed in tomorrow's competitive world; this is the big idea behind writing this book.

'Unlike a karate fighter, who takes sharp, crisp, and aggressive moves against their opponent, a tai chi fighter takes slow, calculated, and thoughtful actions. They move with their opponent instead of going against them. This is how today's business market works. You can't always play on the offensive unless you're a tech giant developing a new innovative product. You have to move in the same direction where your customers go. You need to think beyond sales. You have to follow a holistic approach that provides a Unique Business Contribution (UBC) to your customers – a cornerstone of innovative business methodology named V.S.O methodology or Value Selling Organization I came up with after years of experience that I will later include in this book.

These methodologies have greatly helped my clients and students grow their businesses. The same methodologies described in this book can also help your businesses achieve success quickly.

CHAPTER 1: NEUROPSYCOANALYSIS

If you don't already know this, psychology plays a major role in the consumer buying process. So far, we see how advertisers use subtle marketing techniques that we don't even know but are influencing our buying decisions, leveraging data to tailor these techniques more effectively to individual preferences, embodying the essence of value-based selling.

Microsoft's chosen color theme for Office 365, for example, is calming and inviting. This helps create a sense of comfort in their product and an emotional connection that may encourage you to purchase the Software. This strategic choice, likely informed by data analytics, enhances the product's value by aligning with consumer desires for ease and comfort.

Several factors could be at play here. It could be the physical appeal of an item or the potential cost savings. It may be a fear-based response that triggers you to buy. Regardless, these psychological and neurological processes can influence our purchase decisions. The underlying part of this process includes emotions such as pleasure and comfort, anticipation, and trust. It's not just about the attractive design of a product or the right words in an advertisement. Here, the application of value-based selling, informed by data on consumer behavior, can guide companies in highlighting these emotional triggers more effectively in their sales strategies.

Why do you think Apple has succeeded in making a mark on so many people? It wasn't the first company to build phones, tablets, or even laptops. Sure, they did have an edge with their innovative products, but they did not have the first-mover advantage. Apple's success can also be attributed to its mastery of value-based selling, where it consistently aligns its product development and marketing strategies with its customers' deep-seated values and desires, a strategy supported by extensive data analysis on consumer behavior.

Apple has been a great marketer as much as a brilliant tech company. Over the years, Apple has maintained its reputation by appealing, especially to the young generation, by creating an ecosystem. Apple knows what people want. In the age of Instagram, people want validation and a sense of belonging while promoting individuality. Apple has done just the right job of creating an ecosystem of evangelists. It focuses more on the "experience" of the customer and every consumer touchpoint, whether it's their ads, products, or stores, demonstrating an excellent application of Value-based selling by ensuring every aspect of its offering aligns with the values and expectations of its customers. Apple is a classic example of how using consumer psychology, underpinned by data-driven insights, can make you win.

Similarly, all Apple stores are standardized with the same prices, ensuring that its buyer's consumers are satisfied, i.e., the end consumer. You will never find Apple phones at huge discounts in any retail store because Apple has a controlled distribution process and carefully monitors its pricing across retailers while also maintaining its brand image. This practice exemplifies smart selling through a value-based approach, supported by meticulous data analysis to preserve brand value and customer satisfaction.

Companies must understand how their buyers' and buyers' consumers' brains work. Our brain has two separate portions; one is for decision-making, and the other experiences emotions. The main function of the dorsal prefrontal cortex and orbitofrontal cortex of the frontal lobe is to carry out a visual search, perceive, reason, judge, and make a decision. In the depths of our brain lies the amygdala, hypothalamus, and nucleus accumbent that give our brain the emotional coloring to what it sees and perceives. This is where the pleasure center lies, which decides "what" we like, and Neuroscience helps explain the reason behind such a choice. Thus, our brain plays a huge role in determining our purchases and even helps decide what brand we choose. For example, choosing between Apple and Samsung, not considering the pricing factor, you might choose any of the two depending on what image your brain associates with either of them, a decision-making process that brands can influence through value-based selling, tailoring their messaging and product development based on comprehensive data analysis of consumer behavior patterns.

For example, researchers experimented on brand preference between Pepsi and Coca-Cola, in which the subjects were given two tasting sessions, one of which required the subject to put on a blindfold. When the participants tasted Pepsi without knowing the brand, the "reward center" of the brain was activated, showing that they preferred it. However, when they repeated the Process without the blindfolds, tasting Coca-Cola stimulated the hippocampus, midbrain, and dorsolateral prefrontal cortex (areas for memory and emotion). This could easily be due to the nostalgia the participants experienced due to Coke's brand value and the participants' association with it. The research showed that people like the brand of Coca-Cola more than how it tastes, illustrating the power of brand perception. This key element can be enhanced through value-based selling, where understanding and leveraging such emotional connections, informed by data, can significantly impact consumer preference.

Learning a consumer's behavior regarding their buying patterns answers many questions for companies, but the question is how? Companies can use applied neuroscience, which uncovers how the brain reacts to certain stimuli. As a company, you can use neuroscience to identify a business problem and later provide users with solutions. The most precious thing for big companies in this dynamic age is user data. Tech companies like Facebook are always monitoring and analyzing consumer behavior. They know what you click on during the day and how many times. Based on that, they alter your feed and show you things most relevant to your interests, a strategy that exemplifies the core of value-based selling—using data to understand and cater to consumers' specific values and needs, thereby enhancing engagement and loyalty.

These techniques are also used by firms in other industries, especially retail stores with an online presence. Even B2B businesses now monitor the needs of their client's consumers. For instance, MailChimp, an email marketing platform, noticed that their small business customers had to change their needs. So MailChimp created a new product specifically for these customers, called "MailChimp Solo." In this way, they can stay current with the latest consumer trends and provide their clients with the best products and services, a clear application of value-based selling through data-driven decision-making, ensuring that offerings are always aligned with customer needs and market dynamics.

Keeping neuroscience in mind, they also observed their consumer's behaviors and started giving out "special items" at special prices that were only available for a limited time. This created hype in their customers, and these items sold out quickly. Costco, at large, also remained focused on building a customer experience that would help maintain its sales and keep it at par with its competitors. In this era, companies must learn what their consumers respond to the most. For example, the gen-z age may react more to viral marketing techniques that use gen-z humor. It is all about what appeals to the "pleasure center" of the consumers' brains, and finding that out requires a lot of market.

Buying Process as an Engine for Business

Information overload due to technology and social media has made it difficult for businesses to stand out. With so much noise everywhere, it is becoming increasingly difficult for potential clients and clients' clients to identify your brand. Adopting a value-based selling approach underpinned by data analytics can help businesses tailor their messages to cut through this noise, making their value proposition clear and compelling.

While technology has erased the geographical boundaries that once held businesses back from expanding their customer base to another region, it has also opened more avenues for competition to enter the market. Data-driven market analysis is crucial here, enabling businesses to identify and focus on niches where they can offer unique value.

There are comparatively fewer players in a B2B marketplace, but building strong relationships and understanding who you're selling to is essential. Data analytics can deepen and make this understanding more actionable, enhancing the effectiveness of value-based selling strategies.

In a traditional setting, B2B is a business selling to another business and giving them a smart solution to their problem. For example, a software developer who develops SalesForce software later reaches out to several businesses in an attempt to sell the Software. Here, the principle of value-based selling emphasizes the importance of demonstrating how the Software provides a solution and a strategic advantage, using data to support these claims.

We aim to "explore" the Process of "selling" and how shared value is created as the Software is sold to another business (client) and later helps the end customer (client's client). Data-driven insights into both sets of customers' needs and preferences can significantly enhance the ability to create and communicate this shared value.

The aim is to create shared value, not just economic value or sales profits. It is also the greater good, the value created when an end customer benefits. So, if a company's customer service division buys the sales software, they could help many customers, creating value in society as a whole by helping buyer's consumers. This broader impact can be more effectively achieved and communicated through a value-based selling approach supported by data on customer outcomes.

So, for a software developer, it is important to consider the perception of the client's client and how the Software can help the client's client so our direct client purchases benefit their client. Data-driven decision-making plays a crucial role in understanding these perceptions and designing Software that meets these needs.

In this case, it also becomes essential for the software developer to understand the buying process of both parties to sell their Software. They have to ask, "What is it that my client needs, and how can my clients fulfill their client's needs with the software I am creating?" This understanding is enhanced by analyzing data on both the direct client and the end-user's buying processes and needs.

It sure seems like a long chain, but really, all one has to do is ensure that the business they are offering benefits the client by either helping them cut costs, improve customer relations, or profiting them in some way by automating their business processes and, in turn, allowing their clients to enjoy better service. Value-based selling, informed by comprehensive data analysis, ensures that these benefits are communicated and aligned with client values.

So, what's the secret that could help businesses create shared value? To keep your brand value afloat, knowing your clients and your clients' clients inside out and their journey can provide useful insights into their purchasing patterns and help explain their buying habits. Data-driven insights into these journeys enable a value-based selling strategy that is both effective and efficient.

Understanding the buying process can be extremely rewarding if the business knows how to make the most of each stage and build a targeted strategy for each stage. A business must realize the importance of shared value creation not just for its economic benefit but also for the benefit of all those connected to its client, i.e., buyer's consumers. Adopting a value-based selling approach, underpinned by data-driven decision-making, can significantly enhance this realization and execution.

CHAPTER 2: DEFINING A TARGET AUDIENCE

When defining a target audience, it's important to remember that your audience is more than just a statistic. Your target audience is real people - potential customers you want to engage with and understand your business needs. Utilizing data-driven insights to analyze these needs allows for a more effective value-based selling strategy, ensuring your offerings resonate deeply with your audience.

To truly define your target audience, you need to think about the various characteristics they possess that could help you narrow down their profiles. Look at demographics such as age, gender, and location, but also consider psychographics like interests and values. Consider further factors such as income level or marital status if relevant. Knowing this information will help you create content that resonates better with your target demographic and provide services tailored to their needs. This tailored approach, informed by data, is central to value-based selling, ensuring your services align precisely with what your audience values most.

Another way to understand your target audience is to look at their goals and challenges and ask yourself how your product or service can help them meet those objectives. By understanding their needs, you can create content that speaks directly to them, providing solutions tailored to their specific needs. Data analytics play a crucial role here, offering insights that guide the development of solutions that truly meet the audience's goals.

Finally, it's important to remember that your target audience isn't static - it changes over time as trends emerge and evolve. It's essential to stay up to date with any changes in demographics or psychographics among your customer base so you can fine-tune your marketing messaging and continue engaging effectively with the right people. Adopting a data-driven approach ensures that your value-based selling strategies remain relevant and effective even as your audience evolves.

For instance, let's consider Asana, a project management application. While traditionally, this type of software's target audience was made up of corporate teams, Asana has recently started targeting small businesses and solopreneurs. By understanding that their core customer base was growing to include smaller companies, they were able to adjust their messaging accordingly and market more effectively. This strategic pivot is a prime example of value-based selling informed by data-driven market analysis.

What Emotion Motivates the Target Audience To Purchase?

When it comes to making a purchase, customers are often motivated by either fear or desire. Understanding these emotional drivers through data analysis enables companies to tailor their value proposition, making their offerings more compelling. Fear is the emotion that drives customers to purchase something to alleviate worry or anxiety, while desire motivates them to satisfy an unmet need or aspiration. Companies can enhance their value-based selling approach by aligning products with these emotional needs.

The Gap Between The Market And The Existing Solutions

A market gap is a space in an economic sector or market that is not filled by existing solutions. Identifying these gaps through data analytics allows businesses to innovate and create value-based solutions that meet unaddressed customer needs. Successful companies use market gaps as opportunities to differentiate themselves and offer unique value. Data-driven insights into consumer behavior and emerging trends are key to identifying these opportunities and developing solutions that offer genuine value and stand out in the market.

Let's consider Grammarly, for example. They filled the market gap for grammar and spelling correction tools by offering a comprehensive solution catering to business professionals and casual writers. Their success underscores the effectiveness of using data to identify market needs and develop solutions that deliver significant value, a cornerstone of value-based selling.

By identifying and filling market gaps, companies can create innovative solutions that bring immense value to their customers and differentiate themselves from their competitors. A data-informed, value-based selling approach is crucial to this process, ensuring that companies not only meet but exceed customer expectations, driving growth and success.

The Difference between the Price Of Existing Solutions And The Financial Value Of Your Solution

When investing in a service or solution, many business owners and entrepreneurs are looking for the best deal. Naturally, prospective customers' first question is: what is the price? But it's not all about the price tag; understanding the financial value of a solution is often more critical.

Existing solutions may come with a lower price tag, but often, those solutions don't offer maximum value for the money being spent. Your solution can differ - you offer a higher quality product with superior financial value over time. Increased durability in your product, easier usability, greater scalability, and other benefits pay dividends in the long run. Investing more upfront makes sense if it will bring more power and potential to your customer base - something they can depend on far into the future.

Similarly, when looking at different solutions for businesses or entrepreneurs, there are often additional value-added benefits beyond what is advertised on the price tag. Your solution's financial value should be considered when determining whether or not to invest in it. Investing in a higher-quality product that promises longevity and additional benefits can bring more value for the money being spent, which is why understanding the financial value of your solution is essential.

The Value of Your Solution to The Value Of The Best Product Competing With You.

Delivering a superior product to customers is paramount in the business landscape. Its ability to shine amidst competitors sets a company's offering apart. Businesses must ensure that their services provide valuable solutions, enabling discerning consumers to recognize the advantages of selecting their brand over others. This involves considering the value the solution brings to the client in reaching their business goals and how it positively impacts their clientele, fulfilling their needs and aspirations. The methodology employed by a business should center on the notion that customers make purchasing decisions to attain their objectives while simultaneously considering the value they can provide to their clients.

It would be best if you showcased what makes your product exceptional and why it should be the buyer's first choice. Look at the best-performing competitors on the market today and assess what they offer. Consider how you can refine or offer more value to customers than this—perhaps in terms of convenience, cost savings, product quality, durability, or ease of use—and then make sure those elements are well demonstrated when marketing your solution.

Here are a couple of values that a producer must keep in mind when cross-comparing the values of two different solutions:

1. Understand your end consumers' Point of View

A key element in successful marketing communication is understanding your clients' consumers' points of view. Finding out what the customer needs and wants, their concerns, and how they prefer to receive information is vital when trying to reach them.

Understanding the needs of the clients' consumers means crafting better messaging that resonates with them and creates a connection between them and your client's brand message. By knowing the different perceptions of your true audience, you can create communication strategies that maximize the success of your communication objectives, ultimately creating more impactful results.

For example, ChatGPT provides a revolutionary artificial intelligence solution that any company's finance department could benefit from, and the Process of acquiring such an incredibly useful tool is simple. It starts with the IT department, which plays a key role in providing this AI solution for the finance team. After all, IT professionals are responsible for ensuring the necessary technology is up to date and ready for action. This means that the customer, in this case, is actually the IT department, while those who will experience its actual benefits are, of course, a company's financial staff.

This establishes the customer as the IT department and the target audience (the end-user) as any company's financial staff. Knowing this distinction is the key to creating value that will effectively reach the right people and drive them toward action.

2. Have a complete overview of the organization

A successful business requires more than just good sales and product strategies; everything must be integrated for a 360-degree view.

Take Elon Musk, for example, a famous tech entrepreneur who has successfully launched multiple companies that required an abundance of integrated components from various backgrounds.

Integration can take the form of sales methodology, product methodology, operational framework, or even legal organization. The lesson learned is that to be adequately prepared for scaling up any organization, the founder(s) must have a comprehensive overview of the current landscape and limitations and pre-plan how everything will be integrated once growth begins.

This ensures that owners can make adjustments, pivot if necessary, and accurately forecast what needs to be done to move past current obstacles. A complete overview of the organization will help understand which areas need improvement, expansion, or optimization so that the business can reach its full potential.

3. Develop a business ideology

Shared value creation is a powerful tool that helps organizations create lasting economic and social impact while benefiting their bottom line. It involves developing strategies that build mutually beneficial relationships between business, government, and civil society by connecting organizational goals with societal needs.

By investing in shared value initiatives, companies can develop a unique point of view to bring positive change in the world. This approach emphasizes the importance of collaboration and partnerships, which are essential for progress in creating a sustainable future. At its core, it is an ethical framework for businesses to operate within – one that seeks to maximize profit without neglecting important social needs or disregarding environmental concerns. With this approach, companies can drive meaningful change and make a lasting difference in their communities and beyond.

As a startup CEO, knowing how to create a product that provides value to customers and makes your business successful can be challenging. However, by considering the unique perspective of all stakeholders involved, you can craft an offering that allows your clients and their customers to face any challenge they may encounter. Combining this knowledge enables you to create something truly special - a product that will empower people to take on anything and provide value for everyone involved in the Process. With this approach, scaling up becomes a much easier task.

How far does the concept of shared value creation extend?

The concept of shared value creation goes beyond traditional corporate social responsibility efforts that often focus on mitigating negative impacts or philanthropic endeavors. Instead, it emphasizes the integration of social and environmental considerations into a company's core strategy and operations, recognizing that societal issues can present untapped business opportunities.

By actively seeking out and identifying unsolved social problems, businesses can harness their expertise, resources, and innovative capabilities to design effective and sustainable solutions. This process entails deeply understanding the social context, engaging with stakeholders, and collaborating with diverse partners, including governments, NGOs, and local communities.

Moreover, shared value creation allows companies to develop competitive advantages by differentiating themselves in the marketplace. By identifying and understanding the social dimensions of their target markets, businesses can tailor their offerings to meet customers' specific needs and aspirations, creating a positive feedback loop between social impact and profitability.

Additionally, businesses that actively create shared value can enhance their brand reputation, build trust with stakeholders, attract and retain talented employees, and foster long-term customer loyalty. This, in turn, contributes to a virtuous cycle where societal progress and business success are intertwined.

However, it is important to note that shared value creation is not a one-time accomplishment but an ongoing commitment. Businesses must continually assess and adapt their strategies to address emerging social challenges and evolving stakeholder expectations. Regular monitoring, evaluation, and transparency are crucial to ensure that the intended social impact is being achieved and that business practices remain aligned with the principles of shared value creation.

CHAPTER 3: CUSTOMERS

Finding your end Customers

In the world of business, identifying the driving force behind the process is essential. While organizations often focus on internal decisions such as product development and marketing strategies, the ultimate motivator remains the end customer. Understanding the needs and desires of potential buyers is key to any business venture's success. Leveraging data analytics to gain deep insights into these needs allows for a more nuanced approach to value-based selling, ensuring products and services are precisely tailored to customer demands.

By putting the customer first and tailoring products and services accordingly, organizations can increase their chances of success and ensure long-term sustainability. It's about aligning with what the customer wants and needs, not just the business's objectives. This customer-centric approach, informed by data-driven insights, forms the foundation of value-based selling, where the focus is on delivering genuine value to the customer.

The idea that the customer is at the heart of everything a company does is crucial today. This means adopting the customer's perspective and considering their wants and needs at every process step. For instance, if a customer needs a CRM software solution, understanding this need through data analysis and catering to it can build a relationship of trust and value, exemplifying value-based selling.

In successful business practices, maintaining a direct connection with clients to understand and fulfill their needs requires a collaborative effort. Prioritizing direct communication, supported by data analytics, enables organizations to tailor their offerings more effectively, leading to increased customer satisfaction and success in the marketplace.

In today's economic climate, understanding the needs and wants of buyers is crucial. Adapting product offerings based on data-driven insights into consumer demand can help overcome economic challenges, demonstrating the effectiveness of a value-based selling strategy.

Who Is Your Direct Customer?

The customer is king, especially for direct customers who are the paying customers. Understanding and prioritizing the direct customer's needs, informed by data on their preferences and behaviors, is crucial for any business aiming to implement a value-based selling approach.

What Will Make The End-Customer Buy From My Customers?

In today's market, customers seek value that is meaningful and relevant to their needs. Providing this value, as identified through data analysis, is key to ensuring your customers gain a loyal following. This approach, central to value-based selling, focuses on delivering what the end customer truly values.

Defining value is complex and varies by individual circumstances. The UBC (Unique Business Contribution) method, supported by data analytics, allows businesses to identify and articulate the unique value their products or services offer, enhancing their value-based selling proposition.

Again, the key to success lies in understanding the end user's needs. Working directly with the consumer to identify their unique needs, supported by data, allows businesses to demonstrate the tangible benefits of their product, aligning with the principles of value-based selling.

While requiring preparation and analysis, this concept is about providing consumers with more value for their money by considering their interests and preferences. With data-informed pricing strategies, businesses can optimize profits while enhancing customer satisfaction, a critical aspect of value-based selling.

Ways to Make the Consumer Realize the Value of the Product

Here are some key strategies to make the consumer realize the value of your product:

1. Offer unique benefits—When marketing your products or services, consider how data analytics can uncover the unique needs of your target audience, allowing you to offer something extra that no competitor provides. This could be an exclusive offer or a customized solution. Utilizing data to understand customer needs enhances perceived value, fostering loyalty and advocacy for your brand through a value-based selling approach.

2. Develop user-friendly features – Consumers seek products that are easy to use. Businesses should leverage user data to identify areas where customers struggle and introduce tools like clear tutorials or interactive demos. These data-driven enhancements help customers quickly see the value of your product, boosting their purchase confidence.

3. Demonstrate ROI – Providing customers with concrete figures that show potential savings or benefits from using your product or service is crucial. Use data to demonstrate ROI, illustrating the true value of your offerings and reinforcing the principles of value-based selling.

Innovation Model and Value-based Pricing

Adding an innovation model and value-based pricing, guided by data on unmet needs and the positive impacts of solutions, elevates the concept of creating shared value. This approach encourages companies to look beyond short-term gains and consider the broader social and environmental outcomes their products generate.

Identify new opportunities – An innovation model powered by data analytics can uncover unmet customer needs or societal challenges. Integrating value-based pricing for these new offerings ensures pricing strategies are aligned with the social and environmental benefits provided, creating a compelling value proposition.

Increase customer engagement: Companies can deepen customer engagement by aligning products with customer values and societal benefits and pricing them according to the value they deliver. Customers often pay a premium for products that reflect their beliefs and contribute to a greater purpose.

To implement an innovation model and value-based pricing effectively, consider:

1. Customer research: Use data analytics to deeply understand customer preferences and needs.

2. Value proposition: Craft a unique value proposition that clearly communicates how your offering benefits customers, supported by data.

3. Price: Set prices based on the comprehensive value to customers, including social or environmental benefits, informed by data analysis.

4. Promotion: Promote your offering through data-informed campaigns to reach the audience most likely to value your unique benefits.

Foster collaboration—Collaboration, underpinned by a shared innovation model and value-based pricing, can create partnerships across the industry. Data-driven insights into customer needs and market trends can guide these collaborations, ensuring products and services meet consumers' evolving expectations.

By adopting these strategies, informed by data analytics and focused on delivering genuine value, businesses can meet and exceed customer expectations, driving growth and achieving long-term success in a competitive marketplace.

Drive efficiency

Companies embracing innovation can reduce waste and drive efficiency, resulting in cost savings while lowering their environmental footprint. However, cost savings are not the only benefit of innovation.

When companies adopt value-based pricing coupled with efficiency improvements, they can attract and retain customers.

In addition, companies can look for ways to use data-driven insights to better understand customer needs and behavior. This allows them to optimize their product or service offerings and create tailor-made solutions that meet their customers' specific needs.

How to Implement the Innovation Model and Value-Based Pricing?

The implementation process for adding an innovation model and value-based pricing to improve shared value creation can be broken down into the following steps:

Identify Areas of Opportunity

As the implementation process for a new project begins, it's crucial to focus on the first step: identifying areas of opportunity for shared value creation. Businesses can use data analytics to pinpoint unmet customer needs or societal challenges, laying the groundwork for value-based selling strategies.

Through careful research, businesses can uncover these needs or challenges that may have been previously overlooked. This discovery phase allows innovative thinkers to brainstorm new products, services, or business models that address these issues while creating social and economic value. Data-driven insights ensure that these innovations align with market demands and customer preferences.

By leveraging these areas of opportunity, companies can build a sustainable and successful business while positively impacting their community. Starting your implementation process with data-informed decision-making positions your project for success, taking a crucial step towards creating a better tomorrow.

Develop an Innovation Model

Identifying areas of opportunity is just the beginning of truly creating shared value. The transformation occurs when organizations develop an innovation model that uncovers new opportunities, products, services, and business models. Incorporating data analytics into this model enhances its effectiveness, allowing for the identification of precise areas where innovation can yield the greatest value.

One proven strategy is adopting a design thinking or lean startup approach, which emphasizes rapid experimentation and iteration. This approach, enriched by real-time data feedback, enables organizations to quickly test, learn, and refine ideas, ensuring that the final solution is both innovative and closely aligned with customer needs.

At its core, this approach aims to help organizations quickly test and refine ideas until they find the perfect solution, leveraging data to streamline the innovation process and maximize the impact of their value-based selling efforts.

Align Pricing Strategy with Social and Environmental Benefits

As businesses strive to create new products, services, and business models, there is an increased need to ensure that their pricing strategy reflects the social and environmental benefits they provide.

To do this, market research is crucial in identifying how customers perceive the value of these benefits and what premium they are willing to pay.

By aligning pricing with a product or service's positive impact on society and the environment, companies can increase profits and build a strong reputation as a socially responsible brand. This approach benefits both the business and society as a whole, creating a win-win situation for everyone involved.

Communicate the value proposition.

As consumers become increasingly aware of their impact on the world, businesses must focus not only on the quality and price of their products but also on their social and environmental impact. Leveraging data to understand consumer concerns and preferences is key to effectively communicating a product or service's value proposition in this regard.

Customers want to know how their purchases align with their personal values and contribute to larger issues they care about. This is where businesses can highlight the social or environmental benefits their products provide, utilizing data-driven insights to articulate these benefits compellingly. By doing so, they justify premium prices and increase the customer's willingness to pay.

Monitor and adjust pricing strategy.

Pricing is a crucial aspect of any business; getting it right is essential for success. Adopting a dynamic pricing strategy informed by continuous data analysis allows businesses to remain responsive to customer value perception and market trends. This involves considering customer perception of value, aligning pricing accordingly, and staying attuned to changes in social and environmental priorities. Through this approach, businesses can ensure that their pricing supports shared value creation and remains aligned with customer needs and societal values.

Foster collaboration

Collaboration has become a buzzword in many industries, and for good reason. Companies that work together to create shared value can achieve more than those that go it alone. By bringing together different stakeholders, including customers, suppliers, and partners, companies can tap into a wealth of knowledge and resources to develop products and services that truly meet the needs of their customers.

Whether it's collaborating on new product development or working to improve supply chain efficiency, the benefits of collaborative efforts are undeniable. The key to success is to foster an environment that encourages open communication and collaboration, allowing everyone to share ideas and insights and work together towards a common goal.

Evaluate impact

As the saying goes, "What gets measured gets managed." When running a business, evaluating the impact of your innovation model and value-based pricing strategy is crucial to keeping your company on track.

It's not enough to make an initial assessment and call it a day; regular evaluation is essential in ensuring that you're meeting your customers' needs and living up to your company's values. This may involve gathering feedback through customer satisfaction surveys, examining your product's impact on the environment and society, and carefully monitoring your financial performance metrics.

By regularly assessing your business's performance and making adjustments as necessary, you can stay ahead of the competition and continue to grow and thrive in today's ever-changing business world.

CHAPTER 4: CRAFTING A STRATEGIC PLAN

UBC, Branding, and Market Positioning

In the ever-evolving landscape of business, the rise and fall of companies has been a recurring theme throughout history. Among the multitude of factors that influence a business's trajectory, two components stand out as paramount: strategic planning and branding. These elements possess the power to shape a company's destiny, ultimately determining its success or failure.

In the current era of cutthroat competition, where securing customer loyalty is a coveted achievement, the importance of cultivating a brand that profoundly connects with the intended audience cannot be emphasized enough. Branding is the key to creating an identity that resonates with your target market, helping you stand out among competing rivals.

When done right, branding can profoundly impact a business's bottom line. A well-crafted brand image helps establish trust and credibility in customers' eyes, adding value to a product or service. This, in turn, increases the chances of a successful business venture.

At the same time, it is important to recognize that certain risks are associated with branding. A poorly executed strategy can alienate customers and cause a company to suffer reputational damage.

Understanding UBC Construction

Unique Business Contribution (UBC) refers to the specific set of strengths, capabilities, and resources that a business possesses that sets it apart from its competitors. It represents an organization's unique value proposition and the core competencies that enable it to deliver value to its customers.

Incorporating UBC into strategic planning enables businesses to leverage their strengths to achieve a competitive advantage. By identifying their UBC, businesses can better differentiate themselves from their competitors, establish their brand identity, and develop tailored solutions that meet their customers' specific needs.

It involves assessing an organization's strengths, weaknesses, opportunities, and threats (SWOT analysis) to identify areas where it excels. This information can then be used to develop strategies that leverage these strengths to create a sustainable competitive advantage.

For example, in the tech industry, a company like Apple has a UBC in its ability to design and develop innovative products that seamlessly integrate hardware and software. By incorporating this UBC into their strategic planning, Apple can focus on product development and marketing strategies emphasizing user experience and customer satisfaction. This allows them to differentiate themselves from competitors and establish themselves as a leader in the market.

What is the Difference between the Direct Customer and the End Customer?

As mentioned previously, the direct and end customers are two different types of customers in business.

A direct customer is a customer who purchases a product or service directly from a business. They interact with the business directly and pay the business for the product or service they provide. For example, if a wholesaler purchases goods directly from a manufacturer, the wholesaler is considered a direct manufacturer customer.

On the other hand, an end customer is a customer who uses a product or service but does not purchase it directly from the business. They are the final consumers of the product or service. For example, if a consumer purchases a product from a retailer, they are the end customer of the business that manufactures and sells the product.

Sometimes, the direct customer and the end customer may be the same person. For example, if a consumer purchases a product directly from a manufacturer's website, they are both the direct customer and the end customer. However, in many cases, intermediaries, such as distributors, wholesalers, or retailers, may be involved between the manufacturer and the end customer.

Understanding the difference between the direct customer and the end customer is important for businesses in developing their marketing strategies and determining how to best reach and engage with their target customers.

Building a Marketing Strategy and Plan

A successful marketing strategy is crucial for any business looking to thrive in today's competitive market. By developing a well-planned marketing strategy, businesses can effectively reach their target audience and differentiate themselves from competitors.

To build a successful marketing strategy, businesses must develop a deep understanding of their customers' needs and preferences. This involves identifying the target audience and tailoring marketing messages to both the direct customer and the end customer.

Level 1: Direct Customer

The direct customer is the customer who purchases the product or service directly from the business. To develop a marketing strategy that resonates with the direct customer, businesses must leverage data analytics to identify their needs and preferences, tailor marketing messages to them, and establish brand value and differentiation.

This involves utilizing UBC principles in marketing to direct customers, emphasizing the unique value proposition and core competencies that set the business apart from competitors. Data-driven insights can further refine these tailored solutions, meeting the specific needs of direct customers and solidifying their position as a go-to provider in the industry.

Level 2: End Customer

The end customer is the final consumer of the product or service. To develop a marketing strategy that resonates with the end customer, businesses must use data to understand their needs and preferences, develop marketing strategies to reach them and create brand awareness and resonance.

This involves incorporating UBC concepts into marketing to end customers, emphasizing the unique value proposition that sets the business apart from competitors. By leveraging data to enhance understanding and communication, businesses can create brand awareness and resonance with the end customer, establishing themselves as a trusted provider.

Positioning in the Market

A successful market positioning strategy is crucial for any business looking to establish a strong presence in the market. Utilizing data analytics for market positioning allows businesses to differentiate themselves more effectively and create a unique identity that resonates with their target audience.

What is Market Positioning?

Market positioning refers to creating a specific image or identity in the minds of target customers. Data-driven strategies enable the development of a unique selling proposition that appeals to the target audience's specific needs and preferences, setting the business apart from competitors.

Assessing Current Market Position

To develop an effective market positioning strategy, businesses must first assess their current market position through a comprehensive data analysis of the company's strengths and weaknesses.

Leveraging UBC and Branding for Effective Market Positioning

Businesses must leverage their UBC and branding to effectively position themselves in the market. By emphasizing their unique strengths and capabilities, businesses can demonstrate their value proposition and establish themselves as the go-to provider in the industry. Moreover, by developing a strong brand identity, businesses can create a unique image that resonates with their target audience and establishes loyalty and trust.

Differentiation in the Market

Differentiation is the process of creating a distinct and unique product offering that stands out from its competitors. It can include any combination of attributes, such as price, quality, customer service, product features, or even the brand image itself. Differentiation allows companies to stand out in a crowded marketplace by making them more attractive to customers. By offering a product that is different from the competition, companies can create a competitive advantage and generate more sales and profits.

It can be based on a company's unique business contribution (UBC) or the underlying core value that sets it apart from its competitors. Here are three key areas of differentiation that a company should consider when looking to develop their competitive advantage:

1. Product/Service Features – Does your product or service offer features that are unique or superior to those of your competitors?

2. Quality—Is the quality of your product or service higher than that of the competition?

3. Branding – Is your brand easily recognizable and associated with a specific benefit or niche?

Once you have identified your UBC, it's important to create a clear and effective branding strategy that will help you communicate the value of your product or service to potential customers. Developing an appealing logo, slogan, or website design can be a great way to capture customers' attention and convey your unique value proposition.

It's also crucial to consider how you will effectively communicate your unique value proposition to potential customers. Creating marketing materials that showcase the benefits of your product or service compared to competitors is one effective way to do this. Here are some other tactics for effectively communicating your value proposition:

• Create customer testimonials that highlight the advantages of choosing you over competitors

• Publish case studies that illustrate how customers have been successful with your product or service

- Develop content (blog posts, videos, etc.) targeted towards potential customers to help them understand the benefits of choosing your product or service.

Importance of understanding customer awareness

Understanding customer awareness is crucial for businesses because it allows them to assess how well their target audience knows about their products, services, or brands. Customer awareness is directly linked to customer engagement, brand recognition, and, ultimately, sales and revenue. By understanding customer awareness, businesses can tailor their marketing strategies, communication efforts, and product positioning to reach and engage their target customers effectively.

Methods for evaluating the level of customer awareness

Surveys and questionnaires: Designing and conducting surveys or questionnaires can provide valuable insights into customer awareness. By asking specific questions related to brand knowledge, product awareness, or market understanding, businesses can gauge the level of awareness among their customers.

Interviews and focus groups: In-depth interviews and focus groups allow businesses to engage directly with customers and gain qualitative insights. These methods provide an opportunity to explore customer perceptions, understanding, and awareness levels more deeply.

Web analytics: Monitoring website traffic, user behavior, and engagement metrics can provide an indication of customer awareness. Metrics such as page views, time spent on site, and bounce rates can offer insights into how well customers know and engage with a brand or its offerings.

Social media monitoring: Analyzing social media conversations, mentions, and sentiments related to a brand or industry can provide valuable information about customer awareness and perception. Monitoring social media platforms can help identify trends, customer feedback, and areas of improvement.

Using customer feedback and market research to gauge awareness

Customer feedback and market research play a vital role in assessing customer awareness. Businesses can use techniques such as:

Net Promoter Score (NPS): NPS measures customer loyalty and willingness to recommend a brand to others. A higher NPS score suggests a higher level of customer awareness and satisfaction.

Competitive analysis: Comparing your brand's awareness levels with those of competitors can provide valuable context and insights. Analyzing market share, customer sentiment, and customer preferences relative to competitors can highlight areas where awareness can be improved.

Enhancing customer awareness through targeted marketing efforts

Here are some ways businesses can enhance customer awareness:

Content marketing: Creating valuable and informative content through blog posts, articles, videos, or social media can help increase customer awareness. By sharing relevant and engaging content, businesses can position themselves as industry experts and build brand recognition.

Digital advertising: Utilizing targeted digital advertising campaigns can help increase brand exposure and reach a wider audience. Platforms like Google Ads, social media advertising, and display advertising can be used to specifically target customers based on demographics, interests, and online behavior.

Public relations (PR) and media coverage: Securing media coverage through press releases, media interviews, or partnerships can significantly increase customer awareness. Positive media exposure can help build trust, enhance brand reputation, and reach new audiences.

CHAPTER 5: MANAGING AND HARNESSING STAKEHOLDERS

A Continuous Action Plan

In the grand symphony of business orchestration, the harmonious integration of stakeholders assumes a role of profound significance. As the master conductor of enterprise, the astute leader understands that the true measure of success lies not only in financial gains but in the cultivation of strong and enduring relationships with those vested in the organization's endeavors, guided by a value-based approach and informed by data-driven insights.

Understanding Stakeholder Management

Stakeholder management refers to the systematic and strategic process of identifying, analyzing, and engaging with individuals and groups who have a vested interest or are affected by an organization's activities. Leveraging data analytics enhances the precision of this process, enabling a deeper understanding of stakeholder needs and expectations.

Benefits of Effective Stakeholder Management

Here are four key benefits of effective stakeholder management, each amplified by integrating value-based selling principles and data-driven decision-making:

Enhanced reputation and credibility: By actively managing stakeholders with data-informed strategies, organizations can build trust, credibility, and a positive reputation within their industry and community.

Increased support and cooperation: Data-driven engagement strategies can lead to support, cooperation, and active participation in achieving organizational goals, reflecting the core of value-based selling.

Risk mitigation: Early identification and address of stakeholder concerns, supported by data analytics, can mitigate potential risks and avoid conflicts.

Improved decision-making: Involving stakeholders in decision-making processes, with insights gained from data analysis, can lead to more informed decisions that consider a wide range of perspectives.

Key principles and approaches to stakeholder management

Identify and prioritize stakeholders: Use data analytics to conduct a thorough stakeholder analysis, identifying and prioritizing all relevant stakeholders based on their influence and impact level.

Understand stakeholder needs and expectations: Develop a deep understanding of stakeholders' needs through active communication, feedback mechanisms, and engagement initiatives, all underpinned by data.

Proactive engagement: Engage stakeholders actively through regular communication, consultation, and collaboration, using data to inform these interactions and build relationships.

Tailor communication and engagement strategies: Adapt strategies to suit different stakeholders, ensuring effective interactions, with data guiding the customization of these approaches.

Monitor and evaluate: Continuously monitor stakeholder dynamics and measure the effectiveness of engagement efforts with data analytics, refining strategies over time.

Identifying and Prioritizing Stakeholders

Google's meticulous identification and prioritization of stakeholders to manage its ecosystem and uphold its pioneering brand are exemplary. This process is significantly enhanced by Google's use of data analytics to understand and prioritize the needs and expectations of its diverse stakeholder groups.

Google thoughtfully acknowledges a diverse array of stakeholders, assessing their influence and impact through data-driven analysis. This data-centric approach ensures that Google's engagement strategies are precisely tailored to address the most pressing concerns and opportunities for shared value creation.

Positioning in the Market

A successful market positioning strategy, crucial for establishing a strong market presence, benefits greatly from integrating data analytics to understand target audiences and differentiate from competitors effectively.

What is Market Positioning?

Market positioning involves creating a specific image in the minds of target customers. Data-driven strategies enable the development of a unique selling proposition that resonates with the target audience's needs and preferences.

Assessing Current Market Position

Developing an effective market positioning strategy requires a comprehensive data analysis of the company's strengths and weaknesses, ensuring that real insights inform positioning efforts.

Engaging and Harnessing Stakeholders

At Microsoft, a global technology leader renowned for its cutting-edge software products and services, stakeholder engagement is viewed as an art form that drives innovation and cultivates a positive organizational culture. The company understands the pivotal role of effective communication channels and wholeheartedly embraces the power of engaged employees and collaborative partnerships to propel its success and make a lasting impact.

To bring stakeholders into the fold, Microsoft weaves a tapestry of communication channels that exude transparency and foster regular, meaningful dialogue. From vibrant newsletters that paint a vivid picture of company initiatives to vibrant social media platforms buzzing with real-time updates, the company leaves no stone unturned in ensuring that stakeholders are kept well-informed and active participants in the decision-making processes that shape their collective destinies. Be it dedicated websites offering insights into strategic directions or intimate face-to-face interactions that invite heartfelt conversations, Microsoft opens the floodgates of communication to build trust, promptly address concerns, and forge an environment of collaboration and mutual understanding.

However, Microsoft's commitment to stakeholder engagement doesn't stop at the surface. It dives deep into suppliers' realm, recognizing their significance and the impact their families hold. Carefully orchestrated with purpose and compassion, annual meetings form the threads that strengthen the tapestry of relationships. Within these gatherings, an orchestra of voices harmonizes, exchanging insights, sharing feedback, and aligning their aspirations. Discussions ripple through the air, covering business performance, quality standards, and sustainability initiatives. Yet, these meetings transcend the confines of business, embracing the well-being of suppliers' families as a part of the symphony. Work-life balance, health and safety, and social welfare programs resound in the room, offering a cadence of care. It is through this holistic approach that Microsoft weaves an unbreakable bond, demonstrating unwavering commitment to stakeholder management and fostering profound impacts that extend far beyond the confines of profit margins.

Within the Microsoft family, employees are regarded as treasured stakeholders, and their engagement is nurtured like a delicate garden. A positive work environment becomes the fertile soil that cultivates growth, where camaraderie blooms and individual brilliance is celebrated. The company ensures that every corner exudes a sense of safety and respect, where employees feel seen, heard, and valued. Recognizing achievements becomes an art form, and work-life balance is carefully tended to, allowing the blossoming of well-rounded individuals who bring their whole selves to the Microsoft ecosystem.

But Microsoft's garden doesn't merely flourish through passive admiration. Instead, it is a vibrant ecosystem where employee feedback and participation are the lifeblood that nourishes and invigorates. The company actively seeks the voices of its workforce, weaving a tapestry of opinions through surveys, suggestion programs, and regular feedback mechanisms. Within this symphony of voices, employees find empowerment, a stage where their ideas are heard and their contributions make a difference. From the seeds of participation, a spirit of ownership blossoms, fueling commitment and fortifying the foundation of Microsoft's success.

In this verdant landscape, Microsoft invests in its employees' growth, providing them opportunities to thrive and bloom. Training programs become sunlit pathways that lead to personal and professional development, while mentorship initiatives nurture potential and offer guidance along the journey. Career advancement opportunities unfold like petals unfurling, inspiring loyalty, and strengthening the company's talent pool. Microsoft's commitment to its employees' growth is a testament to the company's dedication to fostering an ecosystem where innovation flourishes, and the symphony of success echoes in every corner.

Managing Stakeholder Expectations

The foundation of effective stakeholder management lies in understanding the expectations of those who hold a stake in the organization. This requires active listening, empathy, and a deep understanding of each stakeholder's unique perspective. Take the example of Microsoft: when Satya Nadella became CEO in 2014, he recognized the need for a strategic shift. Through active listening and engaging in dialogue, he understood the stakeholders' concerns about the company's outdated focus. His strategic vision for a "mobile-first, cloud-first" Microsoft was then communicated and aligned with the expectations of various stakeholders.

Organizations must proactively communicate their goals, values, and objectives to stakeholders, ensuring they are well informed about the company's direction and intentions. Tesla provides a clear example of this practice. Led by Elon Musk, Tesla openly shares its "master plan" with the public, effectively conveying the company's vision and strategic initiatives, thus setting clear expectations and minimizing potential misunderstandings.

To successfully manage stakeholder expectations, organizations must strive to align these expectations with their own activities and capabilities. This alignment necessitates carefully evaluating the feasibility and implications of meeting stakeholder demands. It involves setting realistic expectations, being transparent about limitations, and finding mutually beneficial solutions. Google, a subsidiary of Alphabet Inc., excels in this aspect. Through its annual founders' letter and the "Google I/O" developer conference, the company manages to align stakeholder expectations with its strategic objectives effectively while being transparent about its challenges and future directions.

Lastly, it is mandatory for organizations to address these issues proactively and resolve them fairly and transparently. Salesforce demonstrates this through its annual "Dreamforce" event and its "V2MOM" (Vision, Values, Methods, Obstacles, and Measures) process. The event allows Salesforce to engage with customers, acknowledge their perspectives, and incorporate their feedback into product roadmaps. The V2MOM process helps constructively manage conflicts, reinforce trust, demonstrate commitment to stakeholder satisfaction, and strengthen the overall stakeholder management process.

Integrating Environmental Responsibility

One company that exemplifies integrating environmental responsibility into its operations is the tech giant Apple Inc. Apple has long shown its commitment to minimizing its environmental impact and actively contributing to the preservation of natural resources.

Apple has implemented sustainable practices and policies as a pivotal step in minimizing its environmental footprint. For instance, the company has been continuously striving to reduce its energy and water consumption, with initiatives like powering all its facilities worldwide with 100% renewable energy. Apple also uses recycled materials in its products whenever possible, as showcased in its recent iPhones, which incorporate recycled rare earth elements in the Taptic Engine, reducing the need for mining these resources.

The company also understands the importance of collaborating with environmental organizations and regulatory bodies. Apple is part of the Responsible Business Alliance (RBA), an industry coalition dedicated to corporate social responsibility in global supply chains. It's also worth noting that Apple has partnered with Conservation International, a nonprofit environmental organization, to protect and restore a 27,000-acre mangrove forest in Colombia, demonstrating its commitment to proactive environmental responsibility.

Apple further underlines its environmental responsibility by regularly assessing and reporting its environmental impact and performance. They release an annual Environmental Progress Report, which transparently outlines the company's efforts in reducing its carbon footprint, conserving precious resources, and pioneering the use of safer materials in its products and processes. This report provides stakeholders with a clear insight into Apple's environmental performance and showcases the company's unwavering commitment to environmental stewardship.

CHAPTER 6: BUILDING STRATEGY

Building the Short-Term Startup Strategy under Conditions of Uncertainty

As you stand at the crossroads of your startup's destiny, the world becomes your canvas for creation. Should you venture forth and develop new products, expanding your horizons and captivating untapped audiences? Or perhaps the path lies in deepening your relationships with existing customers, crafting a broader response that resonates with their evolving needs. The possibilities are as vast as the unexplored frontier. Let's uncover the strategic questions that will empower you to conquer the market, surpassing your competitors and claiming your rightful place in the sun.

Should you develop additional products or expand to new target audiences with the existing products?

Strategic contemplation and a willingness to innovate are key as the winds of market dynamics and customer demands shift. Here are a few considerations, informed by value-based selling and data analytics, to help you make an informed decision:

Market demand and competition: Evaluate the demand for your products using data analytics. Expanding your target audience could be strategic if data reveals an untapped customer segment or a growing market. Conversely, in a saturated market, data-driven insights might highlight new product development as a path to growth.

Customer feedback and insights: Use data analytics to gather and analyze customer feedback. A data-driven understanding of their needs can reveal opportunities for new products or features and help identify potential new target audiences that align with your offerings.

Resource availability: Assess your resources, including finances and personnel, through a data-informed lens. Based on data-driven forecasts of required investments and potential ROI, consider whether you have the necessary resources to pursue new product development or market expansion effectively.

Synergies and scalability: Leverage data analytics to evaluate potential synergies between new products and market expansion. Data can reveal existing capabilities that facilitate these initiatives and help assess the scalability of each option, guiding toward the most sustainable growth path.

Risk assessment: Use data analytics for a comprehensive risk assessment of developing new products versus expanding to new audiences. Data-driven risk analysis can inform the decision-making process, balancing potential rewards against the risks.

Embracing a mindset that thrives on the unknown, startups can position themselves for accelerated growth by leveraging data-driven strategies to navigate these strategic decisions. Whether developing new products or expanding to new audiences, data analytics empower startups to make informed choices, revolutionizing industries and rewriting the game's rules.

Should you enter new sectors or provide a broader response to existing customers?

This strategic decision requires a thoughtful approach guided by data analytics and value-based selling principles. Drawing inspiration from Microsoft, startups can leverage stakeholder engagement and collaborative partnerships, underpinned by data-driven insights, to navigate this critical decision-making process:

Assess market potential: Conduct a data-driven analysis of market trends and customer demands. Data analytics can uncover untapped sectors that align with your startup's competencies, positioning you for success in new territories.

Identify complementary sectors: Data analytics can help identify sectors that harmonize with your existing offerings. By entering complementary areas, you minimize risks while expanding your market reach, leveraging data to ensure alignment with your core competencies.

Foster deeper customer relationships: Engage with your customer base, informed by data analytics. Understanding their evolving needs through data can help you tailor your offerings for a more comprehensive solution, reinforcing your market presence and customer loyalty.

Embrace collaboration: Seek strategic partnerships, guided by data analytics, to enter new sectors. Data can help identify potential partners whose offerings complement yours, accelerating growth and unlocking new success avenues.

When is it right to enter into a merger or strategic collaboration?

The prospect of entering into a merger or strategic collaboration introduces both opportunities and challenges for startups navigating uncertain market conditions. Taking a cue from the corporate strategies of Alphabet Inc., Google's parent company, startups should evaluate potential collaborations, shared objectives, and strategic alignment when considering such ventures.

By strategically partnering with organizations that possess complementary strengths and resources, startups can unlock untapped growth potential, access new markets, and foster innovation. A comprehensive assessment of market dynamics, competitive landscape, and long-term strategic objectives should guide the decision to pursue a merger or strategic collaboration.

How do we build an updated value proposition incorporating all of the company's products and services?

Creating an updated value proposition that integrates a startup's products and services into a cohesive narrative requires meticulous planning and strategic alignment. By following the example set by industry leaders like Microsoft, startups should nurture a culture of continuous adaptation and embrace evolving customer needs.

Through an in-depth understanding of customer preferences and market trends, startups can refine their value proposition to provide a comprehensive and tailored response to customer demands. This strategic realignment strengthens the startup's competitive positioning and enhances its appeal in a crowded marketplace.

How to upgrade the product, overcome the competitors, and reach a larger market share?

The pursuit of market dominance and expanded market share necessitates strategic product upgrades and competitive differentiation. By drawing inspiration from Tesla's commitment to innovation and openness, startups can drive product excellence and outpace competitors. This entails leveraging technological advancements, monitoring market trends, and actively engaging with customers to understand their evolving needs.

Startups must adopt an agile approach, continuously upgrading their product offerings and staying one step ahead of the competition. By consistently delivering superior value and meeting customer expectations, startups can capture a larger market share and establish themselves as industry leaders.

What is an Initial Public Offering (IPO)?

An Initial Public Offering (IPO) is the process where a private company offers its shares to the public for the first time in a stock market. It's a significant step that can help a company raise capital, but it requires careful preparation:

Building Trust and Credibility: Before an IPO, a company must prove to potential investors its reliability and success. This can be achieved through consistent performance, transparency in operations, and a solid track record of growth.

Addressing Investor Concerns: Potential investors may have queries or concerns about the company's business model, growth prospects, or management. The company needs to address these concerns proactively, providing detailed information and maintaining open lines of communication.

Showcasing Growth Potential: To attract investors, a company needs to demonstrate potential for future growth. This might involve sharing plans for expansion, new products, or strategies for overcoming potential challenges.

How to prepare for an IPO?

Preparing for an Initial Public Offering (IPO) requires diligent planning and meticulous execution. Startups embarking on this transformative journey should emulate the practices observed in successful IPO processes. Building trust and credibility, addressing potential investor concerns, and showcasing growth potential are paramount.

Just as Salesforce engages customers through its renowned "Dreamforce" event, startups must engage potential investors, demonstrating a compelling investment story and highlighting their unique value proposition. Preparing comprehensive financial assessments, ensuring transparent reporting practices, and aligning organizational objectives with market expectations are critical steps toward a successful IPO.

How to generate significant growth over time beyond the existing organic growth of the company?

Unleashing significant growth potential beyond existing organic levels demands a strategic approach focused on innovation, market expansion, and sustainable practices. By drawing inspiration from Apple Inc.'s commitment to environmental responsibility, startups should explore avenues for growth beyond traditional boundaries. This involves exploring new markets, pursuing strategic acquisitions, and adopting innovative business models.

Additionally, continuously monitoring stakeholder engagement, collecting valuable feedback, and making necessary adjustments to strategies are fundamental in shaping a growth-oriented startup ecosystem. By embracing a forward-thinking mindset and adapting to changing market dynamics, startups can chart a sustained growth trajectory, carving their path toward long-term success.

Should you develop additional products or expand to new target audiences with the existing products?

As the winds of market dynamics and customer demands shift, the answer lies in strategic contemplation and a willingness to break free from the constraints of the ordinary. Here are a few considerations to help you make an informed decision:

Market demand and competition: Evaluate the current market's demand for your existing products. If there is a significant untapped customer segment or a growing market, expanding your target audience could be a viable option. Conversely, if the market is saturated or competition is fierce, developing new products may provide a better opportunity for growth.

Customer feedback and insights: Gather feedback from your existing customers to understand their needs, pain points, and desires. If there are common requests or unmet needs, you can consider developing new products or features that cater to those demands. Similarly, customer insights can help you identify potential target audiences that align with your existing product offerings.

Resource availability: Assess the resources at your disposal, including finances, personnel, and infrastructure. Developing new products requires significant investment in research, development, production, marketing, and distribution. Expanding to new target audiences may also require additional marketing efforts, customer support, and adaptation of your existing products. Consider whether you have the necessary resources to pursue either option effectively.

Risk assessment: Assess the risks associated with both options. Developing new products involves inherent uncertainties, such as market acceptance, development costs, and potential cannibalization of existing products. Expanding to new target audiences may also involve challenges in understanding their unique preferences and adapting your marketing strategies accordingly. Consider the risks and weigh them against the potential rewards.

Shifting the Focus from Inside Out to Outside In

The outside-in approach recognizes that a business's success ultimately lies in its ability to understand and cater to its customers' needs and desires. Instead of starting with a company's products or services and trying to find customers who would be interested in them, the outside-in approach flips the perspective.

It begins by looking from the end-consumer up to the selling organization or production. This means deeply understanding the target market and identifying their primary and secondary needs and wants that may not be adequately met by existing offerings in the market. This approach emphasizes the consumer's perspective, grounding the organization's strategic planning and product development in the real and perceived needs of the consumers.

By shifting the focus to the outside, startups can gain valuable insights into their potential customers' pain points, desires, and preferences. This customer-centric approach allows businesses to tailor their products and services to meet specific demands, creating a more personalized and compelling value proposition. Understanding customers' secondary needs enables startups to identify opportunities for differentiation and innovation and develop new solutions that address those needs more effectively.

This framework emphasizes the importance of customer research, market analysis, and feedback gathering. It requires startups to engage with their target audience, listen to their voices, and observe their behaviors. By actively seeking this outside perspective, startups can gain a deeper understanding of their customers and build stronger relationships based on trust, relevance, and customer satisfaction. This outside-in approach not only helps startups expand their market reach but also fosters long-term customer loyalty and advocacy, creating a sustainable foundation for growth in an ever-evolving business landscape.

Incorporating the outside-in approach also highlights the significance of the value chain. By strategically traversing down the value chain, startups can identify the various touchpoints and stakeholders involved in the customer journey. This holistic view enables them to uncover opportunities for value creation at each stage and enhance the overall customer experience. By aligning their offerings with the needs and wants of customers, from the end-consumer perspective upwards, startups can deliver comprehensive solutions that address a broader range of customer demands, gaining a competitive edge in the market.

Dynamic and Changing Business Strategy

Today's business climate demands that companies be agile and flexible, adapting to constant changes. To support this, the strategy should be dynamic, characterized by:

a. Environmental Scanning: Routinely monitor and analyze the external environment using data analytics to identify emerging trends, market shifts, and potential opportunities or threats. Leveraging data-driven insights enhances the precision of environmental scanning.

b. Competitive Analysis: Regularly assess the competitive landscape with a data-driven approach to understand competitors' strengths, weaknesses, strategies, and offerings. This understanding, informed by comprehensive data analysis, can drive differentiation and highlight areas for improvement.

c. Strategic Planning: Develop a strategic framework outlining long-term goals and objectives, incorporating flexibility and agility to adapt to changing circumstances. Incorporate data analytics to ensure that strategic planning is responsive to real-time market insights and customer needs.

CHAPTER 7: RESULTS-ORIENTED MANAGEMENT

Result-oriented management, also known as outcome-based management, is a management approach focused on achieving specific, measurable results or outcomes. It emphasizes setting clear and achievable goals, defining key performance indicators (KPIs), and aligning all efforts and resources towards achieving those objectives. Result-oriented management focuses on the end product or outcome rather than simply completing tasks or activities.

Importance of Result-Oriented Management

Here are some reasons as to why businesses must consider implementing result-oriented management:

Clarity of Purpose: By defining clear and measurable results, result-oriented management provides a clear direction and purpose for the entire organization or team. Everyone knows what they are working towards and can align their efforts accordingly.

Accountability and Responsibility: Result-oriented management assigns clear responsibilities to individuals or teams to achieve specific outcomes. This creates a sense of ownership and accountability, increasing motivation and productivity.

Effective Resource Allocation: When the focus is on achieving results, resources can be allocated more efficiently and effectively. Managers can prioritize tasks and allocate resources to projects that contribute the most to the desired outcomes.

Measurable Progress: Result-oriented management relies on quantifiable metrics and KPIs, making it easier to track progress towards the desired results. This allows managers to monitor performance and make data-driven decisions.

Adaptability and Flexibility: Result-oriented management encourages adaptability and flexibility in achieving the desired outcomes. If certain approaches are not yielding the expected results, adjustments can be made in real-time to improve performance.

Role of Technology in Result-Oriented Management

In result-oriented management, technology is crucial in enhancing efficiency, productivity, and collaboration throughout the project lifecycle. Organizations can effectively achieve their desired outcomes by leveraging various technological tools and methodologies. Here are some key ways technology supports result-oriented management

Project Management Tools

Utilizing project management software is indispensable to streamline the execution of projects and ensure their successful completion. These advanced tools offer a centralized platform where teams can plan, organize, and track progress with ease. By breaking down complex projects into manageable tasks, project management tools enable teams to allocate resources efficiently and set realistic timelines. This fosters transparency and accountability among team members, as everyone can access project updates and deliverables in real-time. Moreover, these tools facilitate collaboration, allowing team members to work together seamlessly, even if they are geographically dispersed. Through task automation and reminders, project management software empowers teams to stay on track, meet deadlines, and adapt to changing circumstances promptly.

Data Analytics for Tracking KPIs

Result-oriented management requires continuously tracking and evaluating Key Performance Indicators (KPIs). By implementing data analytics tools, organizations can monitor project performance and measure the success of each milestone. Data-driven insights help identify trends, strengths, and areas for improvement. With this knowledge, decision-makers can make informed choices to optimize project strategies and resource allocation. Data analytics also enable early detection of potential issues, allowing teams to take corrective actions before they escalate. Additionally, these tools facilitate data visualization, presenting information in clear and concise formats, making it easier for stakeholders to comprehend and communicate progress.

Agile Methodologies

Agile methodologies, such as Scrum and Kanban, have revolutionized the way projects are managed. These iterative approaches emphasize adaptability and collaboration, allowing teams to respond swiftly to changing requirements and market dynamics. Technology plays a pivotal role in supporting Agile practices. Project management software tailored to Agile frameworks enables the creation of dynamic backlogs, sprint planning, and visual task boards. This empowers teams to prioritize tasks, track progress, and deliver incremental value in short iterations. Agile methodologies foster a culture of continuous improvement, with regular retrospectives driving the enhancement of processes and performance.

Communication and Collaboration Platforms

Effective communication and seamless collaboration are essential for cohesive teamwork. Technology provides various communication tools and collaboration platforms that facilitate real-time interaction among team members, irrespective of their physical location. Features like instant messaging, video conferencing, and virtual meeting rooms enable quick and efficient information exchange. By promoting open communication channels, these platforms foster a strong sense of camaraderie among team members. Moreover, shared document repositories and collaborative editing tools ensure that everyone stays updated on the latest project developments, reducing the risk of miscommunication and duplication of efforts.

Automation and AI-driven Insights

Repetitive tasks can be time-consuming and prone to human error. Technology offers automation solutions that free up valuable human resources and reduce the likelihood of manual mistakes. Automated processes, such as task assignment, data entry, and report generation, improve overall efficiency and productivity. Furthermore, Artificial Intelligence (AI) technologies can analyze vast datasets, extracting valuable insights and patterns that might not be immediately apparent to human analysts. AI-driven insights help make data-informed decisions, mitigate risks, and optimize project outcomes.

Defining the Result

Setting clear and measurable goals is the foundation of result-oriented management. A well-defined goal provides direction and purpose for the organization, department, or project. Without clear goals, it becomes challenging for teams to stay focused and track progress effectively. When setting goals, several best practices should be followed:

Specificity: Goals should be specific and unambiguous. Vague goals make it difficult for teams to know what exactly needs to be achieved, leading to potential confusion and lack of motivation.

Measurability: Goals should be measurable, quantifiable, or observable. This enables tracking progress and determining success or areas for improvement.

Attainability: Goals should be realistic and achievable. Unrealistic goals can lead to frustration and demotivation, while attainable goals drive enthusiasm and commitment.

Relevance: Goals should be relevant and aligned with the organization's overall objectives. When goals are relevant, they contribute directly to the organization's success.

Defining Key Performance Indicators (KPIs)

Key Performance Indicators (KPIs) are specific metrics used to measure progress towards achieving goals. They provide tangible and objective data that indicates how well the organization is performing. Selecting the right KPIs is crucial to ensuring that efforts are focused on the most critical aspects of achieving the desired outcome.

a. Alignment with Goals: KPIs should directly align with the defined goals. Each goal may have multiple KPIs associated with it to measure different aspects of progress.

b. Quantifiable and Measurable: KPIs must be quantifiable and measurable to provide clear data on performance. This enables comparison and analysis over time.

c. Relevance: KPIs should be relevant to the specific goal and the organization's overall strategy. Irrelevant KPIs can lead to wasted resources and efforts.

d. Consistency and Tracking: KPIs should be consistently tracked and monitored to ensure ongoing progress evaluation and timely interventions if needed.

Breaking Down Desired Results

Empowering Quantum Dynamics through Result-Oriented Milestones and Objectives

In the fast-paced arena of cutting-edge technology, Quantum Dynamics, Inc. (Quantum), an exceptional Woman-Owned Small Business, emerges as a trailblazer in Cybersecurity, Information Technology, Logistics, Training, Business Management, and Engineering. Fueled by a rich history of excellence and a passion for responsive service, Quantum embarks on a strategic journey, aligning its mission with the precise needs of its clients. Quantum crafts real-world solutions with an unwavering commitment to innovation, an indispensable force empowering Department of Defense (DoD) operations within the dynamic Joint Interagency Intergovernmental Multinational (JIIM) environment. Their Top Secret-Sensitive Compartmented Information (TS-SCI) Facility Clearance stands as an emblem of their unyielding dedication to security and precision in safeguarding classified information.

Understanding the Ultimate Goal

Step into Quantum's captivating world as they embark on an ambitious cybersecurity odyssey, partnering with a high-profile government agency. Their ultimate goal: to fortify the agency's data citadel with an impenetrable multi-layered security architecture, standing as an indomitable fortress against the relentless tide of cyber threats. Quantum's mission is to empower the agency's operations to thrive without compromise to breathe impenetrable life into their client's vital information infrastructure.

Identifying Critical Success Factors

The pulse quickens as Quantum's experts converge to identify the critical pillars that fortify the project's foundation. Armed with innovative encryption algorithms, they ensure data is rendered unbreakable, even to the most advanced adversaries. Seamless integration of next-gen firewalls is meticulously planned, creating a digital bulwark against intruders. Quantum stays ahead in the cybersecurity dance by embracing the power of real-time threat intelligence feeds. With an unwavering commitment to compliance, they lay a bedrock of trust that their client's sensitive data remains guarded with unyielding rigor.

Defining Specific Milestones

With an air of confidence, Quantum designs a roadmap teeming with milestones, each a triumph in its own right. The project unfurls with a mesmerizing overture, setting the stage for milestone one: an intensive security audit and risk assessment within a mere two months. The tempo quickens as milestone two takes center stage, unveiling the swift yet masterful deployment of firewalls adorned with custom rule sets, a symphony of protection within three months. Next, the conductor's baton signals milestone three, with Quantum orchestrating a harmonious fusion of AI-driven threat detection, providing an agile and sentient guardian in just four months. With anticipation building, the crescendo reaches its peak at milestone four, where Quantum launches a breathtaking display of penetration testing and vulnerability analysis, leaving no chink in the digital armor, all accomplished in five months.

How to Set Incremental Targets?

For the marketing agency mentioned earlier, breaking down the goal of increasing online sales revenue by 20% could involve setting quarterly targets, such as increasing sales by 5% each month or achieving a 15% increase by the end of the second month.

Creating a Realistic Timeline

A realistic timeline is essential for managing expectations and ensuring that the desired result is achievable within a feasible timeframe. Creating a timeline involves considering factors such as available resources, complexity of tasks, and potential challenges.

Assessing Task Dependencies: Identifying task dependencies helps establish a logical sequence of activities and ensures that no essential steps are overlooked.

Resource Constraints: Considering the availability of resources, including human resources, finances, and technology, helps determine if the timeline is achievable.

Contingency Planning: To maintain progress, it is crucial to incorporate buffers in the timeline to account for unforeseen challenges or delays.

Reviewing Past Performance: Evaluating the organization's historical data and past project timelines can provide insights into realistic timeframes for similar endeavors.

Based on the marketing agency's assessment of the client's budget, available marketing channels, and historical data on similar campaigns, they establish a realistic timeline of three months for achieving the 20% increase in online sales revenue. This timeline allows for implementing targeted marketing campaigns, monitoring results, and making data-driven adjustments along the way.

Allocating Resources Effectively

Once the milestones and objectives are set, effective resource allocation becomes vital for ensuring that the organization's efforts and assets are optimally utilized to achieve the desired result. By assessing resource availability and ensuring optimal allocation, teams can enhance productivity and minimize wastage.

Assessing Resource Availability

To allocate resources effectively, organizations need to assess the availability of various resources, including:

a. Human Resources: Identifying the skillsets and expertise required for each milestone and ensuring the right personnel are assigned to specific tasks.

b. Financial Resources: Evaluating the project budget and allocating funds strategically to support different stages of the plan.

Assessing Resource Availability

The marketing agency evaluates the skillsets of its team members to assign the right experts to different aspects of the marketing campaign. They also review the project budget and determine the feasibility of incorporating additional marketing tools and technologies to achieve the desired results.

How to Ensure Optimal Resource Allocation

Optimal resource allocation involves making strategic decisions to utilize resources to maximize productivity and minimize waste. Several considerations play a role in this process:

Prioritization: Identifying critical tasks and allocating resources accordingly ensures that the most important activities receive sufficient attention.

Collaboration and Coordination: Encouraging collaboration and coordination among team members can lead to the efficient use of resources and the sharing of expertise.

Monitoring Resource Usage: Regularly monitoring resource usage helps identify any discrepancies or inefficiencies and enables timely corrective actions.

Flexibility: Being adaptable allows organizations to reallocate resources if circumstances change or new opportunities arise.

Implementing Results-Oriented Management

Results-Oriented Management (ROM) is about understanding its importance and embedding it aptly into the organizational culture. How, then, do we successfully integrate ROM into our operational blueprint? Let's explore

Selecting an Appropriate Management Method

Choosing the right management style can significantly impact the efficacy of ROM. But with so many methods out there, how do we select the one that aligns with our goals and client needs?

Different Management Approaches

The landscape of management approaches is vast and varied. Whether it's participative management, which fosters collective decision-making, or the more directive autocratic approach, where decisions are streamlined from the top, every method has its merits. Results-Oriented Management shines when it can morph and adapt based on these different styles to suit the ever-evolving business milieu.

Let's examine some common management approaches and introduce a few more to provide a broader perspective:

Participative Management: In participative management, leaders actively involve employees in decision-making processes. It promotes collaboration, employee engagement, and a sense of ownership.

Common techniques include brainstorming, surveys, and team meetings to gather input and ideas from employees.

Autocratic Management: Autocratic management involves a top-down approach where decisions are made by a single authority or a small group of leaders. This style is often used in crisis situations or when quick decisions are required. It can be efficient, but if overused, it may reduce employee morale and innovation.

Democratic Management: In democratic management, decisions are made collectively through a majority or consensus vote. This approach fosters a sense of equality and shared responsibility among team members. It can be time-consuming but can lead to high employee satisfaction and commitment.

Laissez-Faire Management: Laissez-faire management is a hands-off approach where leaders provide minimal guidance, allowing employees to have a high degree of autonomy. This approach can be effective in creative fields or when employees are highly skilled and self-motivated. However, it may lack structure and direction in some situations.

Transformational Management: Transformational leaders inspire and motivate their teams to achieve higher performance levels. They often have a clear vision and can influence employees to share that vision, fostering a sense of purpose and commitment.

Tailoring the Method to Client's Needs

Beyond internal alignment, a pivotal part of ROM is tailoring the management approach to resonate with client objectives. Whether a client pursues swift product rollouts or is anchored in innovation, understanding their unique needs and molding your management approach to cater to those specifics can be the linchpin of success in ROM.

The Role of the Manager

The manager is the conductor in the vast orchestra of Results-Oriented Management. But what roles does a manager play to ensure that this mechanism produces the desired results?

Being Present and Attentive

The digital age has redefined the concept of 'presence'. Today, it encapsulates physical attendance and emotional and mental availability. A manager who actively listens, engages, and remains receptive is laying the groundwork for a team where each member feels acknowledged and is thus more driven to deliver results.

Providing Support and Guidance

The journey towards results is strewn with challenges. Managers aren't just leaders; they are guides, mentors, and sometimes, the support system a team needs. By ensuring that the team has the requisite resources, training, and continuous guidance, a manager fortifies their path to achieving set objectives.

Implementing Corrective Actions

Responding to challenges requires strategic thinking, much like a chess player adjusting their tactics in response to their opponent's moves. Corrective actions involve purposeful adjustments aimed at maintaining our trajectory towards successful outcomes.

Much like the diligent captain of a ship, Monitoring and Evaluation steer our Results-Oriented Management, ensuring that we maintain a steady course as we work on achieving our objectives. This process underlines the adaptive nature of our approach, emphasizing continuous improvement and unwavering commitment to achieving results.

Ensuring Client Satisfaction

How well we meet and exceed client expectations not only reflects our proficiency but also cements our reputation as trusted partners. Let's delve into the strategies that ensure client satisfaction remains at the forefront of our approach.

Communicating with the Client

Effective communication is the cornerstone of any successful partnership. Establishing and maintaining open communication channels forms the bedrock of ensuring that our clients' needs are consistently met.

Seeking Client Feedback

Feedback serves as a compass that guides our efforts. Actively seeking input from clients about their experiences, expectations, and concerns not only fosters a collaborative environment but also provides insights to enhance the quality of our services.

Meeting Client Expectations

Ensuring that our deliverables align with clients' vision is paramount. It's about not just meeting but surpassing their expectations.

Delivering Quality Results

Much like a craftsman refining their masterpiece, we painstakingly work to deliver outcomes that reflect our dedication to excellence. Consistently providing results that meet the highest standards is a testament to our commitment to client satisfaction.

Steering Success with Results-Oriented Management

Just like an artist crafting a masterpiece, ROM guides us towards outcomes that go beyond expectations. Beyond the physical, it's the emotional connection that fuels success. The captaincy of achievement rests in the hands of managers who navigate with empathy and guide their teams towards the shores of accomplishment.

Netflix - Leveraging Results-Oriented Management for Innovation and Growth

Netflix, founded in 1997 as a DVD rental-by-mail service, has transformed into a global streaming entertainment powerhouse. Its innovative business model and unique company culture, which emphasizes Results-Oriented Management (ROWE), have played a pivotal role in its success. This case study explores how Netflix leverages ROWE to drive innovation, foster a culture of accountability, and achieve exceptional growth.

Background

Netflix's journey from a DVD rental company to a streaming giant is a testament to its ability to adapt, innovate, and disrupt traditional industries. As of my last knowledge update in September 2021, Netflix's ROWE-inspired approach has significantly driven its success.

Results-Oriented Management at Netflix

Netflix's approach to ROWE is not limited to flexible working hours or remote work. Instead, it revolves around a set of core principles that align with achieving results:

Freedom and Responsibility: Netflix operates on the principle of giving employees substantial freedom and autonomy. Instead of micromanaging how and when employees work, the focus is on results. The responsibility of delivering outcomes balances this freedom.

No Vacation Policy: Netflix is famous for its policy of not tracking vacation days. Employees are trusted to take time off as needed to recharge, and this policy is underpinned by the belief that responsible employees will ensure their work gets done.

Unlimited Parental Leave: Netflix offers unlimited paid parental leave during the first year after a child's birth or adoption. This policy reflects the company's commitment to supporting employees in maintaining work-life balance.

Transparent Information Sharing: Netflix maintains transparency in sharing financial and strategic information with employees. This helps employees understand the company's goals and how their work contributes to its success.

Leveraging ROWE for Innovation

Netflix's ROWE-inspired approach fosters an environment where innovation can thrive:

Focus on Creativity: By empowering employees to manage their time and prioritize tasks, Netflix creates a conducive environment for creativity. Engineers, designers, and content creators have the flexibility to explore and innovate.

Risk-Taking: Netflix encourages calculated risk-taking. With a focus on results, employees are more willing to experiment and take risks, which is essential for creating groundbreaking content and technology.

Data-Driven Decision-Making: Netflix's decision-making process is centrally based on data analytics and A/B testing. This data-driven approach helps fine-tune content recommendations, personalization, and user experiences.

Challenges and Future Directions

While Netflix's ROWE approach has been a key driver of its success, it is not without challenges. Balancing freedom with accountability can be complex, and Netflix continues to evolve its policies to address emerging issues.

Netflix's journey from a DVD rental service to a global streaming giant is a testament to its innovative culture and Results-Oriented Management approach. By focusing on results, empowering employees, and fostering a culture of creativity and responsibility, Netflix has disrupted the entertainment industry and achieved remarkable growth. While challenges persist, the company's commitment to ROWE principles continues to drive its ongoing success in the ever-evolving streaming landscape.

Adobe - Empowering Innovation and Creativity through Results-Oriented Management

Adobe is a global leader in software solutions for creativity, document management, and digital marketing. Adobe's journey to success is deeply rooted in its Results-Oriented Management (ROWE) approach, which emphasizes outcomes over traditional work structures. This case study explores how Adobe leverages ROWE principles to foster innovation, engage employees, and maintain its position as a creative technology powerhouse.

Background

Founded in 1982, Adobe has been at the forefront of digital innovation, providing tools and services that empower creatives and businesses worldwide. Adobe's commitment to ROWE has been instrumental in driving its culture of innovation.

Results-Oriented Management at Adobe

Adobe's ROWE philosophy revolves around several key principles.

Flexibility and Trust: Adobe strongly emphasizes trust and flexibility, allowing employees to manage their own work schedules and locations. This approach is grounded in the belief that responsible employees will deliver results regardless of where or when they work.

Clear Expectations: Adobe sets employee expectations, defining key performance indicators (KPIs) and goals aligning with the company's strategic objectives. Employees understand their expectations and are empowered to achieve those outcomes.

Continuous Feedback: Adobe encourages regular feedback and performance discussions between managers and employees. This ongoing dialogue helps employees stay aligned with company goals and make necessary adjustments to achieve results.

Work-Life Integration: Adobe promotes work-life integration rather than strict separation. This allows employees to strike a balance between personal and professional commitments, resulting in higher job satisfaction and well-being.

Fostering Innovation Through ROWE

Adobe's commitment to ROWE principles has played a pivotal role in fostering a culture of innovation:

Empowering Creativity: Adobe's creative software tools, such as Photoshop and Illustrator, are used worldwide. ROWE principles empower Adobe's own creative teams to explore new ideas, experiment, and develop cutting-edge software solutions.

Cross-Functional Collaboration: ROWE encourages cross-functional collaboration and knowledge sharing, enabling employees from different departments to come together, share insights, and develop innovative solutions.

Continuous Improvement: Adobe's culture of feedback and accountability promotes continuous improvement. Employees are encouraged to challenge the status quo and seek better ways to achieve results.

Results and Impact

Adobe's commitment to ROWE has yielded significant results:

Innovative Product Development: Adobe consistently releases innovative software updates and new products, such as Adobe Creative Cloud, which have been instrumental in maintaining its leadership in the creative software industry.

Employee Engagement: Adobe is consistently recognized as a top employer and has a high level of employee satisfaction. ROWE principles have contributed to a motivated and engaged workforce.

Market Leadership: Adobe's software solutions continue to dominate their respective markets, making it a global leader in creative software, document management, and digital marketing.

Challenges and Future Directions

While Adobe's ROWE approach has been largely successful, it's not without challenges. Maintaining a balance between flexibility and accountability requires ongoing effort and adaptation to changing work environments.

Adobe's success story as a creative technology powerhouse is closely tied to its commitment to Results-Oriented Management. By emphasizing results over traditional work structures, fostering innovation and collaboration, and maintaining a culture of flexibility and trust, Adobe continues to thrive in a competitive industry. As the workplace evolves, Adobe's dedication to ROWE principles positions it to remain a leader in creative technology and a beacon of innovative workplace practices.

Fostering Innovation through ROWE

GitHub's commitment to ROWE principles has had a profound impact on fostering innovation within the company:

Empowering Developers: GitHub's platform empowers developers to collaborate on projects, share code, and experiment with new ideas. This collaborative spirit aligns with ROWE principles and encourages innovation in software development.

Open Source Contributions: GitHub has become a hub for open source contributions, enabling developers worldwide to collaborate on projects that drive technological advancements.

Results and Impact

GitHub's commitment to ROWE has led to remarkable results:

Platform Growth: GitHub's platform hosts millions of repositories and is the preferred platform for developers globally, underscoring its leadership in code sharing and collaboration.

Innovation in Development Tools: GitHub continues to innovate by introducing features such as Actions, Discussions, and Codespaces. These tools empower developers and organizations to streamline their workflows and enhance productivity.

Developer Community: GitHub's vibrant developer community is a testament to its success in fostering collaboration, creativity, and innovation in software development.

Challenges and Future Directions

Despite its achievements, GitHub faces challenges in maintaining a balance between flexibility and accountability as it continues to grow. Adapting to developers' evolving needs and the changing landscape of software development is an ongoing endeavor.

GitHub's success as a leading platform for software development and collaboration can be attributed, in part, to its commitment to Results-Oriented Management principles. By emphasizing results over rigid work structures, fostering innovation and collaboration, and maintaining a developer-centric culture, GitHub continues to shape the future of software development. As the technology landscape evolves, GitHub's dedication to ROWE positions it to remain a key player in empowering developers and organizations worldwide.

CHAPTER 8: BUILDING STRONG FOUNDATIONS BEFORE HIRING

Imagine constructing a skyscraper. Without a deep and resilient foundation, even the most magnificent design is susceptible to collapse. Similarly, in the vast skyline of businesses, hiring the right talent is akin to adding floors to this skyscraper.

However, before those floors materialize, the base must be robust and primed to support the impending growth. This chapter delves into setting the stage for successful staffing by emphasizing the necessity of a solid infrastructure. The journey isn't merely about identifying the right people—it's about ensuring your organization is equipped to welcome and nurture them.

Let's navigate through the criticality of carving out clear values, articulating a compelling mission, understanding your target audience, and outlining distinct roles. Each of these components acts as a supportive pillar, reinforcing the foundation of your organization ensuring that as you integrate talent, your business stands tall and steadfast against challenges.

Defining Your Values and DNA

Establishing a clear set of values and understanding your company's DNA can act as your compass. These are not mere words on a wall or slides in an induction presentation; they are the principles that guide behavior, inspire innovation, and build a sense of community.

Identifying Your Core Values as an Individual or Team

In the tech realm, where collaboration is a cornerstone, and each individual potentially holds the key to the next disruptive idea, recognizing one's core values is paramount. Start by asking:

What drives me or us forward each day?

Which principles do I or we refuse to compromise on, even if it means losing out on an opportunity?

What do I or we want our legacy in the tech world to be?

Once identified, these values become the guiding light in collaborative efforts, ensuring that everyone on the team is aligned in their mission, from developing a groundbreaking algorithm to streamlining a user experience.

Reflecting on the Company's DNA and Culture

Your company's DNA is its unique fingerprint in the tech industry. It encapsulates the essence of what makes your organization different from the myriad of startups and tech giants out there. Reflect on:

The origins: What challenges were faced during the inception of the company? How have those experiences shaped the organization's approach to problem-solving?

The interactions: How do team members communicate and collaborate? Is it a hierarchical structure or a flat, democratic one?

The innovations: What kind of projects does the company gravitate towards? Is it about pushing boundaries or refining existing solutions?

The answers to these questions will help map out the genetic makeup of your company's culture. This DNA becomes a part of your brand, attracting like-minded talents and clients who resonate with your ethos.

The Role of Values in Decision-Making and Company Identity

In the tech industry, where the pace is frenetic, and the stakes are high, values act as a stabilizing force. They guide strategic decisions, from which partnerships forge, and help you reach the kind of talent you need to onboard. A company that prioritizes open-source, for instance, will make decisions vastly different from one that fiercely guards its intellectual property.

Moreover, these values are a beacon for your company's identity in a crowded marketplace. They help clients, partners, and potential hires understand not just what you do but why you do it. In an era where company culture is often as significant as the products or services offered, your values become a compelling differentiator.

Case Study: Google's Commitment to "Don't Be Evil"

Google, now a part of Alphabet Inc., is well-known for its commitment to the principle "Don't Be Evil." This value has been a guiding force for the company since its early days. It represents the importance of ethical behavior and responsible technology use. Google's founders, Larry Page and Sergey Brin, incorporated this principle into their corporate culture.

Actionable Steps

Identify core values: Google's core value of not harming users or the world was foundational.

Apply values in decision-making: Google used "Don't Be Evil" to guide decisions on product development, partnerships, and business practices.

Tesla's Vision for Sustainable Transport

Tesla, led by Elon Musk, has a clear purpose beyond profit - accelerating the world's transition to sustainable energy. This vision guides Tesla's mission to produce electric vehicles and renewable energy solutions. Tesla's North Star is about selling cars and addressing climate change through innovation.

Actionable Steps

Define a clear purpose: Tesla's purpose is to accelerate the transition to sustainable energy, addressing a global challenge.

Create a mission statement: Tesla's mission is to make electric vehicles and sustainable energy accessible to all.

Set strategic goals: To achieve its mission, Tesla sets specific goals, such as producing affordable electric cars and expanding renewable energy solutions.

Harmonizing the Heartbeats: Merging Personal Beliefs with Corporate Ethos

In the vibrant realm of technology, where individual brilliance often interlaces with collective endeavor, there's an understated symphony at play. It's the rhythm created when an individual's personal values resonate with the overarching values of the company they're a part of.

Begin this introspective journey by holding a mirror to your own beliefs and ideals. Assess how these personal tenets sync with the value system of your organization. Are you a staunch believer in open-source, and does your company champion transparency and collaboration in the same vein? Or perhaps you hold sustainability dear, and you're part of an enterprise pushing the envelope in green technologies. This alignment isn't just about personal satisfaction; it's about ensuring the energy you bring to the table finds a harmonious echo in the company's larger chorus.

The magic of this harmony can't be overstated. When individual and company values are in sync, it fuels an organic and robust company culture. It fosters an environment where teams don't just work together; they believe together. This collective belief system becomes the wind beneath the wings of innovation, pushing boundaries and elevating benchmarks.

However, in instances with discordant notes—value misalignments—it's essential not to turn a deaf ear. Instead, strategies must be employed to bridge these value gaps. Maybe it's through open dialogues that bring varied perspectives to the table. It could also be through initiatives and training that acquaint teams with the company's core values and their importance. By actively addressing these gaps, companies not only ensure a more cohesive work environment but also build trust, signaling that every voice, every value, holds significance.

To thrive in the tech world isn't just about having the brightest minds or the most innovative products. It's about ensuring that the heartbeats of every individual align, creating a rhythm that propels the organization toward unparalleled success.

Structuring Better Teams: Elevating the Hiring Journey with Feedback Magic

Elevating the Candidate Experience

Just as a skyscraper's design must consider the comfort of its occupants, a thoughtful hiring process prioritizes the candidate experience. Feedback mechanisms allow organizations to gain valuable insights into how candidates perceive their journey, enabling them to make meaningful improvements. This, in turn, ensures that candidates feel respected and valued throughout the process.

Practical Measures for Companies:

Implement candidate feedback surveys at key touchpoints in the hiring process.

Regularly review feedback data to identify areas for enhancement.

Actively respond to candidate feedback and communicate changes made based on their input.

Data-Driven Decision-Making

Feedback provides a treasure trove of data and insights that guide evidence-based decisions. It serves as a compass, helping organizations navigate the complexities of candidate assessment. By analyzing feedback, trends and patterns emerge, enabling organizations to adapt and refine their hiring strategies.

Guiding Insights for Companies

Collect and analyze feedback systematically, looking for patterns and trends.

Use feedback data to inform decision-making in areas such as candidate selection and process optimization.

Continuously iterate on your hiring process based on the insights gathered from feedback.

Promoting Fairness and Bias Reduction

Just as a skyscraper must be structurally sound, a fair hiring process is essential. Feedback mechanisms assist in identifying potential biases in recruitment. By scrutinizing feedback data, organizations can ensure their hiring decisions are impartial, fostering an equitable hiring environment.

Actions to Foster Fairness

Implement bias-awareness training for hiring teams.

Regularly audit feedback data to identify and address any bias in the hiring process.

Establish clear and standardized evaluation criteria to minimize subjective judgment.

Alignment with Company Values

A skyscraper stands tall when its components align seamlessly. Similarly, feedback helps assess whether candidates align with a company's values and culture. It ensures that new hires possess the necessary skills and fit harmoniously within the organization's ethos.

Steps to Align with Values

Define and communicate your company's values and culture clearly to candidates.

Use feedback to evaluate candidates' alignment with these values.

Incorporate value-based questions into interviews and assessments.

Fostering Communication and Transparency

Transparency is akin to the strong pillars supporting a skyscraper. Providing feedback to candidates, regardless of the outcome, promotes open communication. It maintains a positive employer brand and nurtures goodwill in the job market, much like a beacon in the skyline.

Ways to Promote Communication

Establish a feedback process that includes clear and respectful communication with candidates.

Provide feedback promptly after each stage of the hiring process.

Encourage candidates to share their feedback on the recruitment experience as well.

Empowering Candidate Development

Just as a skyscraper's blueprint evolves, feedback empowers candidates to grow and adapt. Constructive feedback, even for those not selected, offers insights into strengths and areas for improvement. It becomes a catalyst for their career development.

Empowerment Strategies for Candidates

Offer personalized feedback to candidates, highlighting areas for improvement.

Provide resources or suggestions for candidates to enhance their skills and qualifications.

Encourage candidates to reapply in the future and track their progress.

In a nutshell, feedback mechanisms are the scaffolding that upholds the hiring process. They enhance the candidate experience, facilitate data-driven decisions, reduce bias, align candidates with company values, promote transparency, and empower candidate development. Much like the sturdy foundations discussed in Chapter 8, feedback mechanisms ensure that the hiring journey is successful and continuously evolving and improving. So, let the magic of feedback elevate your hiring process to new heights!

Diversity and Inclusion

Building a diverse and inclusive workforce in the tech industry is essential for innovation, creativity, and equitable opportunities. However, it comes with its own set of challenges. Here are some common challenges companies might face when laying the foundation for hiring for diversity and inclusion, along with potential solutions to overcome them:

Challenges

Bias in Hiring: Unconscious biases can affect hiring decisions, leading to the preference for candidates who share similar backgrounds or characteristics with existing employees.

Solution: Implement blind recruitment practices, where candidate information such as name, gender, and ethnicity is removed from resumes during the initial screening process. Training hiring managers and interviewers to recognize and mitigate bias is also crucial.

Limited Candidate Pool: In some cases, companies may struggle to find diverse candidates, especially for specialized tech roles.

Solution: Expand recruitment efforts by partnering with organizations that promote diversity in tech, attending diverse job fairs, and leveraging online platforms to reach a wider audience. Encourage employee referrals and offer referral bonuses to incentivize current employees to refer diverse candidates.

Inclusive Culture: Retaining and fostering an inclusive environment can be challenging even after hiring a diverse workforce.

Solution: Create a culture that values diversity and inclusion from the top down. Establish employee resource groups (ERGs) or affinity groups to provide a sense of community and support for underrepresented employees. Conduct regular diversity and inclusion training for all employees and leadership.

Inclusive Policies: Outdated policies or practices may inadvertently exclude certain groups from participating fully in the workplace.

Solution: Regularly review and update policies to ensure they are inclusive and do not discriminate against any group. Seek input from employees, especially those from underrepresented backgrounds, to identify areas where policies may need revision.

Measurement and Accountability: Without clear metrics and accountability, it can be difficult to track progress in diversity and inclusion efforts.

Solution: Set clear diversity and inclusion goals and regularly measure progress. Hold leaders accountable for meeting these goals and tie performance evaluations and compensation to diversity and inclusion outcomes.

Solution: Invest in ongoing education and training for HR professionals and employees involved in diversity and inclusion initiatives. Attend conferences, seminars, and webinars to stay informed about the latest trends and research.

Airbnb's Cultural Attraction for Hosts

Airbnb focuses on attracting hosts who align with the company's cultural values of hospitality and community. The company showcases success stories of hosts who have created unique and welcoming guest experiences, highlighting the vision of a global community of travelers.

Actionable Steps

Align with company growth: Airbnb attracts hosts who want to be part of a global community, which aligns with the company's growth strategy.

Showcase company vision: Success stories and testimonials from hosts illustrate Airbnb's vision for its community and hospitality culture.

Prioritize onboarding and integration: Airbnb provides resources and support to help hosts integrate into the Airbnb community and deliver exceptional guest experiences.

Charting the Fluid Blueprint: Embracing Evolution in Tech Teams

In the vast ocean, staying still means getting left behind. Just as captains must adjust their sails to ever-changing winds and currents, organizations must adapt to the shifting dynamics of the market to remain on course.

At the heart of this voyage is the practice of diving deep to regularly reassess roles and responsibilities. As the waves of business ebb and flow, roles within an organization might need to evolve. By keeping a finger on the pulse of these changes, businesses ensure they're always sailing smoothly, with each crew member playing their part to perfection. This consistent check ensures that the ship—our metaphorical business—runs like a well-oiled machine, optimizing both efficiency and team morale.

However, the view inside the ship isn't the only perspective that matters. Keeping a keen eye on the horizon—representing the broader business environment—is equally vital. The business seascape is dotted with emerging islands of opportunity, shifting tides of customer preferences, and, occasionally, storm clouds of new competitors. Navigating these waters requires a vigilant crew, always ready to adjust their course based on the signs the seascape offers.

Nonetheless, spotting an island or a storm isn't enough. A seasoned sailor knows that adaptation is the true North Star. This philosophy rings especially true when it comes to building and nurturing a crew—our staffing strategy. The evolving demands of our journey might require different talents and skills at different times. Being ready to onboard new sailors, train them for the journey, or even reassign roles ensures that the ship is always prepared for whatever the seascape has in store.

Microsoft's Agile Transformation

Microsoft transformed its software development teams, transitioning from traditional waterfall methodologies to agile practices. This adaptation allowed Microsoft to respond more flexibly to market changes and customer feedback, improving product development.

Actionable Steps

Periodically review roles: Microsoft periodically evaluated and adjusted roles within its software development teams to match agile principles.

Monitor market changes: The company closely monitored market trends and customer needs, adjusting its product development strategies accordingly.

Be flexible in team composition: Microsoft made efforts to onboard individuals with expertise in agile methodologies and foster a culture of adaptability within its teams.

Anchoring the Odyssey: Nurturing Teams from Bedrock to Zenith

The dividends of investing time and resources in building a robust foundation before hiring are manifold.

Such a foundation ensures that every new member joins not merely as an employee but as a stakeholder in a shared vision. It safeguards against the turbulence of the tech world, allowing for growth that is both rapid and rooted.

Beyond the immediate benefits, a long-term perspective paints an even more compelling picture. Through an unwavering commitment to values alignment and role clarity, organizations don't just survive; they thrive. They evolve into entities where individuals find purpose, collaboration sparks innovation, and challenges morph into stepping stones for greater accomplishments.

Steering through the ever-shifting currents of the tech landscape requires more than skill—it demands vision, foresight, and an anchored foundation. It is this foundation, meticulously laid and continuously nurtured, that transforms organizations from fleeting entities into timeless legacies. As teams converge and diverge, adapt, and evolve, it is this bedrock of shared values and clarity of purpose that becomes their guiding star, illuminating paths unknown and journeying from today's achievements to tomorrow's dreams. In the grand panorama of tech evolution, these foundational threads weave stories of enduring brilliance.

Case Study: Facebook's Focus on Values and Culture

Facebook strongly emphasizes its company culture and values, emphasizing openness, collaboration, and impact. The company's commitment to these principles has helped it attract and retain top talent and foster innovation.

Actionable Steps

Invest in values alignment: Facebook actively assesses candidates for cultural fit and alignment with the company's values during the hiring process.

Continuously nurture the foundation: The Company regularly conducts culture assessments and surveys to ensure alignment with its values and make necessary adjustments.

Maintain a long-term perspective: Facebook's leadership maintains a long-term focus on values and culture, viewing them as essential for enduring success.

CHAPTER 9: LEADERSHIP IN THE DIGITAL AGE

At its core, leadership embodies the art of guiding a team toward a shared vision, fostering collaboration, and inspiring collective achievement. On the other hand, management entails efficiently organizing resources and processes to achieve specific goals.

In the digital age, where technological advancements redefine workplace dynamics, leadership takes on a multifaceted role. Beyond the conventional traits of vision and guidance, leaders in the digital era must navigate a landscape influenced by rapid technological evolution, requiring a nuanced understanding of how to harness technology for effective collaboration, innovation, and adaptability.

In this era, leadership transcends conventional boundaries, embracing a dynamic fusion of strategic thinking, emotional intelligence, and a keen understanding of the profound impact of technology on organizational dynamics. Let's unravel the intricacies of leadership in the digital age, offering insights into the skills, strategies, and mindsets required to navigate and excel in this technologically driven professional landscape.

The Impact of Manager Presence: Beyond Physical Proximity

While physical presence is undoubtedly important, the true essence of effective leadership goes far beyond merely being in the same room. A manager's presence should encompass emotional and intellectual availability, fostering a culture of open communication and empowerment within the team. In this era, understanding and enhancing manager presence is critical to leveraging the full potential of a team.

Understanding the Spectrum of Manager Presence

Manager presence can be envisioned as a spectrum, with physical presence as the foundational element. However, to truly harness the potential of their team, managers need to transcend this basic level of engagement.

Physical Presence: A manager's physical presence is the baseline requirement. It means showing up at the workplace and being visible to the team. This presence can provide a sense of stability and direction to the team.

Emotional Availability: Emotional presence delves into the manager's ability to connect with team members on a personal level. It involves empathetic listening, showing genuine care, and being attuned to the emotional needs of the team. For instance, a manager offering support to a team member during a personal crisis demonstrates emotional availability.

Intellectual Availability: A manager's intellectual presence revolves around fostering a culture of continuous learning and growth. It includes engaging in discussions, encouraging diverse perspectives, and challenging the team intellectually. For instance, a manager who encourages brainstorming sessions or invites team members to contribute their ideas promotes intellectual availability.

Examples of Manager Presence in Action

From attentive, active listening that fosters trust to intellectually stimulating feedback sessions driving innovation, these instances showcase how emotionally and intellectually available managers enhance team dynamics and performance.

Active Listening: When a team member expresses their concerns or ideas, an emotionally available manager listens attentively, asks clarifying questions, and validates their feelings. This creates trust and openness within the team.

Feedback Sessions: Intellectually available managers regularly conduct feedback sessions encouraging team members to share their thoughts on projects, processes, and team dynamics. This fosters open communication and leads to process improvements and innovation.

Strategies for Enhancing Manager Presence

Here are some strategies for enhancing Manager Presence:

Scheduled One-on-One Meetings: Regular one-on-one meetings with team members provide an opportunity for managers to connect on a personal level. These meetings can discuss career development, address concerns, or simply check in on the team member's well-being.

Open-Door Policy: Encourage an open-door policy where team members can approach the manager with their ideas, questions, or issues at any time. Make it clear that their voices are valued and their concerns will be addressed promptly.

Lead by Example: Show your team what it means to be emotionally and intellectually available by modeling the behavior yourself. Share your experiences and insights, and let your team see that you are committed to continuous learning and growth.

A manager's presence goes beyond just occupying space in the workplace. It encompasses emotional and intellectual availability, creating an environment where team members feel valued, heard, and empowered.

By actively incorporating these elements into their leadership style, managers can foster a culture of open communication, collaboration, and innovation, leading to improved team performance and a more vibrant and engaged workplace.

As we delve into leadership in the digital age, these principles of manager presence remain foundational, providing a solid framework for navigating the complexities of a technologically driven professional landscape.

Celebrating the Range of Personality: Embracing Both Extroversion and Introversion

Discussions often revolve around extroversion and its impact on leadership and team dynamics in the pursuit of understanding and optimizing workplace dynamics.

While extroversion is undoubtedly an intriguing facet of personality, focusing exclusively on it can inadvertently marginalize the strengths of introverted leaders and employees.

Let's strike a balance by acknowledging the significance of extroversion while also shedding light on the valuable contributions of introverted individuals. Furthermore, we'll explore strategies to create an inclusive environment that honors diverse personality types.

Extroversion and Its Influence

Extroverted individuals are often celebrated for their sociability, assertiveness, and outgoing nature. They tend to excel in roles that require networking, public speaking, and team leadership. These qualities can be highly valuable in certain workplace scenarios, but it's essential not to overlook the strengths of introverted individuals.

Strengths of Introverted Leaders

Here are a few key strengths of introverted leaders:

Deep Thinkers: Introverted leaders are known for their ability to dive deep into complex problems, analyze data, and make well-informed decisions. Their reflective nature often leads to well-thought-out strategies.

Empathetic Listeners: Introverts excel in active listening, creating a space where team members feel heard and valued. This empathy can foster strong bonds and trust within the team.

Effective One-on-One Communication: Introverted leaders often shine in one-on-one interactions, providing team members with personalized guidance and support.

Case Studies of Empowering Givers

Case Study: The Mentorship Maven - Sarah's Journey

Meet Sarah, a mid-level manager whose intrinsic motivation to mentor others sets her apart. Recognizing the immense potential in Sarah's giving nature, the organization made a strategic move by appointing her as the official mentorship program coordinator. This decision not only acknowledged and celebrated Sarah's passion but also paved the way for a cultural shift within the company.

Sarah's journey as the Mentorship Maven is characterized by a seamless alignment of her personal values with the organizational mission. By officially entrusting her with the responsibility of coordinating the mentorship program, the company not only harnessed her natural inclination to help others but also magnified the impact of her efforts. This empowerment acted as a catalyst, unlocking Sarah's untapped potential as a mentor and facilitator.

In her new role, Sarah became a central figure in fostering a robust mentorship culture within the organization. She organized workshops, networking events, and training sessions, creating a supportive ecosystem for both mentors and mentees. This initiative had a profound ripple effect, improving employee engagement, skill development, and knowledge sharing.

Sarah's case exemplifies how organizations can transform a giver's passion into a strategic asset, fortifying their internal culture's fabric. By aligning her skills with a designated role, Sarah not only continued her altruistic endeavors but also inspired others to embrace the spirit of mentorship, creating a more collaborative and growth-oriented workplace.

Challenges and Safeguards

Here are a few key challenges and safeguards for leaders to consider when looking into managing the Givers of the organization:

Burnout Prevention: Givers are at risk of burnout due to their selflessness. Encourage them to set boundaries and take time for self-care. This can be done through wellness programs and awareness campaigns.

Recognition and Rewards: Implement a reward system that acknowledges and celebrates givers. This can include bonuses, public recognition, or career advancement opportunities.

Transparency and Accountability: Ensure that givers' contributions are transparent and that the organization maintains accountability in recognizing their efforts. This can be achieved through regular evaluations and feedback channels.

In an organization that values and empowers its givers, a culture of generosity and collaboration thrives. By shining a spotlight on the unsung heroes who consistently give, we not only enrich the workplace environment but also unleash the untapped potential for innovation and success.

Through case studies, recognition, and proactive safeguards, organizations can create an ecosystem where givers are celebrated, valued, and protected, ultimately fostering a culture of giving that benefits all.

Bridging Departmental Divides

Introduction: Traditional mentorship often operates within departmental silos, limiting the potential for cross-departmental collaboration and knowledge exchange. However, a groundbreaking approach is gaining momentum—appointing a manager as a mentor for a new hire who is not from their department. This innovative concept breaks down barriers and fosters a culture of collaboration, creating a win-win scenario for both the mentor and the mentee. In this section, we will delve into the unique role of managers in this mentorship model, provide guidelines for its effective implementation, and explore the potential challenges and benefits of this cross-departmental approach.

The Manager as Mentor

In this approach, a manager from one department becomes a mentor to a new hire from another department. Their role extends beyond the traditional manager-employee relationship and encompasses:

Guidance and Support: The manager-mentor provides guidance on navigating the company culture, understanding organizational goals, and adapting to the new department's dynamics.

Cross-Departmental Insights: They facilitate the mentee's integration into the new department by sharing insights and connections across departments, helping the mentee build a broad network.

Career Development: The mentor helps the mentee set career goals and provides advice on skills and experiences needed for future advancement.

Guidelines for Effective Mentorship

Embarking on a mentorship journey requires a thoughtful and strategic approach to ensure its success. The following guidelines provide a framework for cultivating a meaningful mentorship experience that fosters growth, communication, and mutual development.

Clear Objectives: Define clear objectives for the mentorship, outlining what the mentee seeks to gain and how the mentor can assist in achieving those goals.

Regular Communication: Encourage regular meetings between the mentor and mentee to discuss progress, challenges, and growth opportunities.

Feedback Loop: Create a feedback loop that enables both parties to provide input on the effectiveness of the mentorship and make necessary adjustments.

Understanding Customer and Employee Needs

An inclusive management approach is pivotal for fostering a deeper and more nuanced understanding of both customer and employee needs. By embracing diversity within the leadership team, organizations are better positioned to connect with a broad spectrum of stakeholders. This diverse leadership is instrumental in devising strategies that resonate with a wider audience, ensuring that a variety of perspectives and needs are considered in the decision-making process.

Incorporating data-driven decision-making into this inclusive framework further amplifies its effectiveness. Organizations can uncover hidden patterns, preferences, and challenges that might not be immediately apparent by analyzing data from various customer segments and employee feedback. This data-centric approach allows for the more accurate tailoring of strategies to meet the specific needs of different groups, enhancing the alignment with diverse needs.

Such alignment is crucial for boosting customer satisfaction by delivering products and services that truly meet the diverse market expectations. Similarly, employee engagement is significantly enhanced when individuals feel their unique perspectives are valued and reflected in organizational practices. This not only fosters a more inclusive workplace culture but also drives innovation by harnessing a wide range of ideas and solutions.

Ultimately, the combination of an inclusive management approach with data-driven decision-making contributes significantly to organizational success. It enables companies to be more adaptive, responsive, and innovative, meeting the evolving needs of their customers and employees in a dynamic business environment. This holistic approach ensures that strategies are inclusive and grounded in empirical evidence, leading to more sustainable and impactful outcomes.

Strategies for Inclusion

Strategic initiatives are essential to fostering an inclusive management environment. Here, we delve into pivotal strategies that transcend traditional boundaries, aiming to raise awareness and actively cultivate an atmosphere of inclusion.

Training Programs

Implementing comprehensive diversity and inclusion training programs is a cornerstone for creating an inclusive management environment. These programs should focus on raising awareness and provide practical tools for recognizing and mitigating unconscious biases. Training sessions can foster a culture of respect and understanding among team members.

Mentorship Initiatives

Mentorship programs can play a pivotal role in fostering inclusivity by providing guidance and support to individuals from underrepresented groups. Establishing mentorship initiatives allows for the transfer of knowledge, skills, and opportunities, contributing to the professional growth of all team members. This, in turn, bolsters a sense of belonging and equality within the organization.

Diversity Recruitment Efforts

Creating a diverse workforce begins with intentional efforts in the recruitment process. Organizations should actively seek candidates from diverse backgrounds, ensuring a broad representation in the talent pool. This involves reevaluating recruitment strategies, utilizing diverse hiring panels, and promoting job opportunities in a variety of channels to reach a more extensive and varied audience.

Leadership Styles: Adapting to the Changing Tides

Leadership is a dynamic and multifaceted concept that transcends the constraints of a one-size-fits-all approach. In this comprehensive exploration, we will delve into various leadership styles, dissecting their advantages and disadvantages, and unravel the art of adapting these styles to different scenarios and organizational needs.

Leadership Style Overview

Some important leadership styles that can facilitate an organization in achieving its goals include:

Transformational Leadership

Transformational leadership is characterized by leaders who inspire and motivate their teams to achieve beyond expectations. They encourage creativity and innovation, fostering a sense of collective purpose. Pros include heightened employee engagement and a culture of continuous improvement. However, potential cons may arise from overemphasizing vision at the expense of day-to-day operations.

Democratic Leadership

In a democratic leadership style, decision-making is a collaborative effort involving input from team members. This approach promotes a sense of inclusivity and shared responsibility. The pros include a high level of employee satisfaction and a wealth of diverse ideas. On the flip side, the decision-making process can be time-consuming, and in certain situations, a lack of clear direction may emerge.

Servant Leadership

Servant leaders prioritize the well-being and development of their team members. They lead by serving, focusing on the needs of others before their own. This style fosters a positive organizational culture and strong interpersonal relationships. However, challenges may arise if the leader's selflessness is perceived as a weakness, potentially impacting decision-making efficiency.

Empathy, Motivation, and Social Skills

Exploring the intricacies of empathy, motivation, and social skills, we unveil strategies for leaders to cultivate and apply these essential components of emotional intelligence. Through real-world examples and actionable practices, leaders can elevate their ability to connect, inspire, and collaborate effectively within their teams and beyond.

Technology's Influence on Management

Advancements in technology have revolutionized management practices, fundamentally altering the way businesses operate. Tools enabling remote work have blurred geographical boundaries, fostering global collaborations and redefining traditional office structures.

Moreover, the advent of data analytics has empowered managers to make informed, data-driven decisions, optimizing processes and strategies. Communication channels have evolved, becoming more diverse and instant, enabling seamless interactions across distances.

Technology has become a cornerstone in decision-making processes, offering real-time insights and predictive analytics. This enables managers to navigate complexities and uncertainties with a clearer understanding of trends and patterns.

Concurrently, communication has transcended physical barriers, with tools like video conferencing and instant messaging enhancing collaboration and fostering a cohesive work environment, regardless of team members' physical locations. Staying adaptable to technological advancements in management has become imperative, as innovation continues to shape the way businesses function.

Embracing these changes allows leaders to stay agile, leveraging emerging tools to streamline operations, enhance productivity, and foster a culture of continuous improvement. Remaining open to technological evolution fosters resilience, enabling businesses to thrive in dynamic landscapes and adapt swiftly to ever-changing market demands.

As technology advances further, its symbiotic relationship with management will continue to redefine strategies, empower decision-makers, and pave the way for innovative solutions, ultimately driving success in the modern business world.

Digital Leadership Skills for Success

Leading in the Digital Age requires mastering adaptability, data literacy, and seamless digital communication - essential skills for navigating the ever-evolving landscape of technology-driven success.

Adaptability in an Ever-Changing Landscape

In the tech-driven world, adaptability emerges as a critical skill for managers. The rapid evolution of technology demands leaders who can swiftly acclimate to new tools, methodologies, and market dynamics. Embracing change and fostering an organizational culture that encourages flexibility becomes imperative.

Data Literacy as a Prerequisite

Managers must possess a significant level of data literacy to effectively decipher and utilize the information available. In today's data-rich environment, understanding data analytics and drawing meaningful insights from complex datasets is not just an advantage; it's a necessity. This capability equips leaders to make strategic decisions that are aligned with the organization's objectives and informed by a deep analysis of relevant data.

Data analytics within a data-driven approach enables managers to identify trends, patterns, and anomalies within large volumes of data, turning raw data into actionable intelligence. This process involves the application of statistical analysis, predictive modeling, and machine learning techniques to interpret customer behavior, market dynamics, and operational efficiency. By harnessing these insights, leaders can anticipate market changes, optimize operational processes, and tailor strategies to meet the evolving needs of their target audience.

Furthermore, data analytics empowers managers to quantify the impact of potential decisions before they are made, reducing uncertainty and risk. It allows for the simulation of different scenarios, providing a clearer picture of possible outcomes and their implications for the organization. This analytical rigor ensures that decisions are not based on intuition alone but are supported by empirical evidence and a thorough understanding of the data.

Incorporating a data-driven approach into strategic planning and decision-making processes fosters a culture of continuous improvement and innovation. It encourages managers to question assumptions, challenge the status quo, and seek data-backed solutions to complex problems. Moreover, it democratizes decision-making by providing a common framework and language for discussing insights and strategies, enhancing collaboration across different levels of the organization.

Ultimately, integrating data analytics into management practices enhances the organization's agility and competitiveness. It enables leaders to confidently navigate the complexities of the modern business landscape, making informed decisions that drive growth, enhance customer satisfaction, and achieve long-term success.

Mastering Digital Communication

Communicating effectively across various platforms and mediums is pivotal in a digitally connected world. Managers must convey ideas succinctly, foster engagement, and ensure clarity in digital exchanges. Skills in written communication, virtual presentations, and leveraging digital tools for effective communication become indispensable.

Developing Competencies for the Future

Equipping leaders with a culture of continuous learning, innovation, and collaboration cultivates a tech-savvy management force poised to lead in the ever-evolving landscape of technology-driven progress.

Continuous Learning and Skill Development

Empowering managers to continuously learn and upskill in technological advancements ensures their proficiency in navigating the digital frontier. Providing access to training programs, workshops, and resources fosters a culture of continuous improvement.

Embracing Innovation and Experimentation

Encouraging a mindset of innovation and experimentation allows managers to explore novel solutions and technologies. Creating a safe space for trying new approaches fosters creativity and positions the organization at the forefront of technological advancements.

CHAPTER 10: BUSINESS PROCESS MANAGEMENT

In the sphere of operational optimization, process comprehension is paramount. Envision workflows intricately calibrated to customer-centric principles, where inception stems from the end-user's viewpoint. This section delves into the nuances of our core processes, their alignment with corporate objectives, and the data-driven KPIs steering their efficacy.

Coordinated by interdisciplinary squads, we navigate the meticulous documentation safeguarding seamless execution and error mitigation, ensuring each maneuver remains finely attuned to customer requisites.

Process Identification

In the domain of process identification, the operational blueprint undergoes a transformative approach. Rather than initiating the processes from an internal standpoint, businesses embark on a journey that begins and revolves around the customer. Picture it as sketching a map: our journey commences by discerning and comprehending our customers' specific needs and aspirations. This understanding acts as the guiding compass, steering the company's subsequent steps. By starting from the customer's perspective, business processes should intricately be aligned to fulfill their precise desires and expectations.

But the focus isn't confined to the present; it extends far into tomorrow's horizon. The radar should be finely tuned to monitor market fluctuations and capture customers' voices. This ongoing vigilance isn't just about understanding the now; it's the crystal ball that forecasts the future. It enables firms to not only identify potential paths that lie ahead but also decipher the prerequisites these paths demand. By doing so, organizations seamlessly intertwine foresight with the evolving desires of their customer base.

The magic happens at the nexus of what customers seek today and what they will yearn for tomorrow. This intersection becomes a strategic vantage point—a juncture where the needs of the present converge with the predictions of the future. It's akin to constructing a roadmap, not just showing where the business stands currently but also acting as a guiding light toward where it needs to be.

This fusion of insights doesn't just stop at envisioning; it's a continuous process of strategic evolution. A blend of current customer insights with predictive analytics is mandatory to craft processes that are adaptable, flexible, and resilient. This agility ensures firms remain ahead of the curve, perpetually prepared to steer their operations in accordance with the ever-evolving scenery of customer expectations and market dynamics.

Such an approach isn't static; it's an ongoing evolution. It's a commitment to continuous improvement, adapting the strategies and operations based on the dynamic needs and trends in the market. By embracing this paradigm, companies ensure that the processes stay in perfect harmony with customer desires and foster an environment of perpetual growth and innovation.

Input and Output Analysis

When it comes to unraveling the intricate components of primary business processes, businesses find their starting point rooted in an in-depth understanding of consumers. These processes, akin to a well-oiled machine, begin their journey with inputs sourced from extensive consumer insights. These insights serve as the raw material, the foundation on which the entire operational structure is built. They form the nucleus, guiding the decisions and actions at every turn, emphasizing the critical role of data-driven decision-making in navigating the complexities of modern markets.

With these invaluable inputs at hand, operations transform them into finely tailored solutions and products. It's a meticulous process, similar to an artisan sculpting a masterpiece, where advanced data analytics tools and techniques play a pivotal role. These outputs are not just products; they're finely crafted offerings that bear the fingerprint of consumer insights, shaped and refined through the lens of data-driven analysis. Their creation is purposeful, ensuring that they aren't just commodities but solutions engineered to directly address and satisfy the nuanced needs of our customers, as identified through rigorous data examination.

Transitioning to the strategic decision-making arena, these processes are the compass in determining the trajectory for acquiring or introducing new products and services. Here, the modus operandi is deeply intertwined with understanding the pulse of the consumers, facilitated by sophisticated data analytics platforms. Businesses delve into their needs, aspirations, and voids in the market terrain, not just at a surface level but through a comprehensive dive into their world. This involves listening to their feedback and studying market trends with a discerning eye, all through the application of data analytics.

This analytical depth, powered by data-driven decision-making, allows firms to discern market gaps and identify opportunities where their offerings can make a meaningful impact. It's not merely about introducing products to follow trends; it's about meticulously filling voids, bridging gaps, and delivering solutions that align seamlessly with what consumers truly seek, as revealed by data insights. This approach ensures that new acquisitions or introductions aren't shots in the dark but calculated moves founded on a deep-rooted understanding of the clientele and the market ecosystem they inhabit, all illuminated by the clarity and precision that only a data-driven approach can provide.

By leveraging data analytics in this way, businesses can enhance their agility, responsiveness, and effectiveness in meeting consumer demands. This not only bolsters their competitive edge but also fosters a culture of innovation and customer-centricity, ensuring that every strategic move is informed by a thorough understanding of the market dynamics and consumer preferences.

Alignment with Corporate Goals

One of the paramount considerations lies in assessing the synergy between each business process and the overarching Unified Business Concept (UBC). This conceptual framework serves as the lodestar, orienting them towards unwavering customer satisfaction and nimble responsiveness to market dynamics. Every facet of the operations undergoes meticulous scrutiny to ascertain its resonance with this guiding principle.

At the heart of this evaluation is each process's profound impact on the customer journey and its pivotal role in propelling the strategic imperatives forward. We delve deep into the core of every operational cog, deciphering its contribution to elevating customer experiences and advancing organizational objectives. This discerning scrutiny allows businesses to navigate and thrive within the competitive landscape.

In the pursuit of operational excellence, companies employ a multifaceted array of criteria and metrics to gauge the efficiency and precision of these processes in augmenting customer experiences. This compass encompasses a spectrum of metrics – from the quantifiable dimensions of customer satisfaction scores, response times, and market share growth to the qualitative insights derived from intricate feedback loops. These metrics serve as a litmus test, guiding businesses in unveiling the efficacy and potency of the endeavors to enrich the customer journey.

The amalgamation of these assessments constitutes the compass, steering firms inexorably towards crafting experiences that resonate deeply with their patrons while bolstering their standing in the market. This relentless pursuit of aligning processes with the ethos of Corporate UBC encapsulates its commitment to delivering unparalleled value and innovation to its clientele.

Data-driven KPIs

In pursuing operational excellence, businesses adopt a multifaceted approach by employing diverse criteria and metrics to evaluate their operational efficiency. This approach includes a comprehensive range of metrics designed to assess various performance dimensions, integrating both traditional and innovative measures to ensure a holistic view. Notable among these are Customer Satisfaction scores, which provide insights into customer contentment response times, which gauge the speed of customer service, and Market Share growth metrics, which are crucial for understanding competitiveness and market position. The inclusion of data-driven Key Performance Indicators (KPIs) such as these allows for a dynamic and responsive evaluation process, adapting to the evolving business landscape and customer expectations.

The outcome of this evaluative process is a thorough assessment of operational performance, enriched by the strategic use of data-driven KPIs. These KPIs serve not only as benchmarks for current performance but also as indicators for future improvements, guiding strategic adjustments and operational enhancements. Furthermore, the evaluation extends beyond quantitative dimensions to incorporate qualitative insights, ensuring a balanced and nuanced understanding of operational success.

Quantitative metrics encompass customer satisfaction scores, response times, and market share growth, providing measurable indicators of operational efficiency and customer engagement. On the qualitative side, feedback loops are established to gain nuanced insights into operational endeavors, capturing the voice of the customer and other stakeholders to inform continuous improvement. This dual approach, bolstered by data-driven KPIs, serves as a litmus test for the efficacy and potency of operational strategies, facilitating informed decision-making based on a holistic understanding of operational performance.

Crafting customer experiences is a strategic imperative, and data-driven insights are pivotal in this endeavor. The integration of data-driven assessments, particularly through the application of KPIs focused on customer experience and satisfaction, is essential for steering business decisions toward creating experiences that resonate deeply with patrons. By systematically analyzing customer interactions, feedback, and satisfaction levels, businesses can identify areas of excellence and opportunities for enhancement, tailoring their offerings to meet and exceed customer expectations.

The overarching purpose is to deliver unparalleled value and innovation, reinforcing the commitment to the Corporate Unified Business Concept (UBC) - the guiding principle directing operations towards customer satisfaction and responsiveness to market dynamics. Businesses can achieve a competitive edge through the strategic application of data-driven KPIs, fostering a culture of excellence that prioritizes customer satisfaction and operational efficiency. This commitment to leveraging data for continuous improvement and strategic decision-making underscores the importance of a data-centric approach in achieving operational excellence and crafting superior customer experiences.

Here are a few key metrics businesses may employ in order to boost productivity and drive a maximum return on efforts:

User Engagement Metrics

User Engagement Metrics stand as a critical category of data-driven Key Performance Indicators (KPIs). These metrics are specifically designed to track and analyze user interactions with a tech product or platform, offering valuable insights into the platform's overall appeal and stickiness. Examples of User Engagement Metrics include Daily Active Users (DAU), Monthly Active Users (MAU), and User Retention Rate. By assessing these metrics, tech companies can understand the level of user involvement and the platform's ability to retain its user base over time.

Churn Rate

Another indispensable KPI for tech companies is the Churn Rate, a metric that gauges the percentage of customers who discontinue using a product during a specified period. This metric serves as a fundamental indicator of customer satisfaction and the effectiveness of customer retention efforts. The Churn Rate is calculated by dividing the number of customers lost during a specific period by the total number of customers at the beginning of that period, multiplied by 100. A lower Churn Rate signifies better customer retention and sustained business viability, making it a crucial metric for strategic decision-making.

Product Performance Metrics

Tech companies also heavily rely on Product Performance Metrics to assess the efficiency and reliability of their technological offerings. These metrics provide insights into the quality of the user experience and the overall health of the technology infrastructure. Examples of Product Performance Metrics include Load Time, measuring the speed at which a product or service responds to user interactions; Uptime Percentage, indicating the availability of the technology without interruptions; and Error Rates, reflecting the frequency of technical glitches or malfunctions. Monitoring and optimizing these metrics are crucial for ensuring a seamless and reliable user experience, thereby contributing to the overall success and competitiveness of the tech company.

Documentation and Execution Chain

Regarding business processes, the Documentation and Execution Chain assumes a critical role in steering operations toward efficiency, precision, and, ultimately, customer satisfaction. This section delves into the strategic process of summarizing trigger points and seamlessly integrating supporting information throughout the execution chain, emphasizing its vital role in ensuring smooth process execution and minimizing errors.

Summarizing Trigger Points and Supporting Information

The meticulous documentation of the execution chain aims to identify key trigger points where customer interaction or feedback significantly influences the process. These critical junctures serve as guiding markers, enabling the evolution of the process based on real-time insights derived from customer engagement.

Within the documentation, supporting information is a comprehensive assembly of crucial elements such as market data, customer journey maps, and process flowcharts. Market data offers a contextual understanding of external influences; customer journey maps illuminate the user experience, and process flowcharts visualize the sequential progression of operational tasks. The integration of these elements forms a robust foundation for informed decision-making at every phase of the execution chain.

Ensuring Smooth Process Execution and Minimizing Errors

The detailed documentation serves as a strategic guideline for smooth process execution, providing a roadmap for all stakeholders involved. By summarizing trigger points, the documentation offers a clear and structured overview of the execution chain, facilitating a shared understanding among team members. This clarity aids in aligning each step with the nuanced needs and expectations of the customer.

The documentation ensures meticulous alignment of each step in the execution chain with customer needs. By capturing the essence of customer interactions and feedback at trigger points, the process becomes inherently customer-centric, fostering a proactive approach to addressing evolving requirements. This alignment is fundamental to delivering products and services that resonate with customers more deeply.

By including supporting information, the documentation becomes a tool for anticipating potential bottlenecks and challenges. Market data and customer journey maps provide insights into possible hurdles, allowing organizations to address issues before they escalate proactively. This foresight contributes to a more agile and responsive approach to process management.

The detailed documentation is instrumental in minimizing errors throughout the execution chain. By providing a comprehensive understanding of each phase, potential pitfalls can be identified and mitigated. This proactive stance toward error reduction increases operational efficiency, ensuring processes unfold precisely and accurately.

Create by Dell-E

CHAPTER 11: AUGMENTING SALES

How AI, VR, and Future Tech Are Revolutionizing the Game

The sales world is undergoing a radical transformation driven by the game-changing power of cutting-edge technologies. Forward-thinking businesses are no longer confined to traditional methods but are embracing Artificial Intelligence (AI) and Virtual Reality (VR) to revolutionize their sales strategies and market presence. This burgeoning market, projected to reach a staggering $165.91 billion by 2030, paints a clear picture: embracing these innovations is no longer optional; it's essential for future success.

According to Statista, the AR and VR market has seen significant growth worldwide, with countries like China and the United States leading the way in terms of innovation and adoption. This statistic underscores the rapid acceleration of these technologies, offering a glimpse into their transformative potential for the sales landscape.

AI in Sales: Personalization and Efficiency

Artificial intelligence (AI) is emerging as a powerful tool for sales organizations seeking to enhance their teams' performance. While its adoption within sales processes remains underutilized at 37% across all organizations, 50% of high-performing sales teams leverage AI to gain a competitive edge.

It's important to note that leveraging AI shouldn't be construed as a path to fully automating sales roles. AI tools are most effective when used strategically to complement and empower your sales team, not replace them. By automating repetitive tasks and streamlining workflows, AI frees up valuable time and resources for your team to focus on what they do best: cultivating meaningful customer relationships and closing deals.

Imagine your sales team armed with AI's insights and efficiency. They can spend less time manually entering data and generating reports and more time analyzing customer behavior, crafting personalized pitches, and building trust with potential clients. This ultimately leads to increased sales productivity, improved customer satisfaction, and a more competitive edge for your organization.

What is meant by AI in Sales?

Artificial intelligence (AI) transforms the sales landscape by simplifying and optimizing processes through trainable algorithms. Software tools harnessing these algorithms leverage large datasets to uncover powerful insights. These AI-powered solutions are designed to empower sales teams, saving time and driving efficiency to sell more effectively.

AI algorithms possess the unique ability to learn from and apply data in diverse ways:

Automating repetitive tasks and making data-driven decisions: Tedious paperwork and manual analysis are streamlined, freeing up valuable time for strategic activities.

Predicting customer behavior and suggesting personalized strategies: Historical and current data fuel actionable insights, enabling tailored approaches that resonate with individual customers.

Engaging with customers intelligently: AI-powered chatbots and virtual assistants offer responsive support, enhancing the customer experience and freeing up human representatives for more complex interactions.

Why should AI be implemented in a business?

Statistics paint a stark picture: inside sales reps dedicate only 33% of their time to active selling, with the remaining consumed by administrative tasks and meetings. AI presents a compelling opportunity to reclaim this wasted time and fuel sales success.

Business leaders recognize this potential. A recent Salesforce study reveals that AI ranks among the most valuable sales tools in 2022, a significant climb compared to 2019. Forrester further predicts an exploding market for AI-powered platforms, reaching $37 billion by 2025.

Beyond hype, AI's practical applications are transformative

Adaptive Strategies: AI empowers teams to seamlessly adjust to increasingly sophisticated buyers and evolving purchase journeys.

Personalized Engagement: Leverage insights gleaned from vast data points to target different customer personas with highly relevant messaging and offers.

Real-Time Insights: AI grants immediate access to accurate and consolidated data, ensuring teams operate with a clear and unified understanding of opportunities.

Multi-Platform Tracking: Today's sales efforts span numerous channels. AI helps centralize and track prospects across all touchpoints for comprehensive reach.

Sales professionals report an accelerated pace of digital transformation, with technology needs evolving rapidly in just the past three years. AI is a crucial tool to navigate this shifting landscape, equipping teams with the agility and data-driven insights needed to thrive.

Benefits of Leveraging AI in Sales

The fusion of artificial intelligence (AI) and automation is demonstrably driving revenue growth in sales. A comprehensive Hub Spot survey reveals that 61% of sales teams exceeding their goals leverage automation, solidifying its impact as a strategic pillar. This trend goes beyond isolated instances; high-growth companies actively integrate AI into their strategies, as highlighted by The Hinge Research Institute study.

But the benefits extend far beyond mere revenue figures:

Enhanced Efficiency: Consulting firm Deloitte reports that efficiency reigns supreme as the primary motivator for AI adoption, with 33% of implementing teams experiencing significantly streamlined processes.

Reduced Administrative Burdens: A McKinsey study pinpoints that nearly 30% of sales tasks are ripe for automation using existing AI-powered technology. Reclaim valuable time by offloading these tedious activities.

Accurate Sales Planning & Prediction: Over half of salespeople consider sales forecasts the most critical data gleaned from analytics tools. AI and automation empower you to elevate the sales planning process through insightful AI-powered data and predictive intelligence.

Increased Job Satisfaction: Surprisingly, AI holds positive implications for team morale. A 2022 Deloitte survey found that 82% of respondents believe AI enhances their job performance and satisfaction.

By strategically integrating AI and automation, sales teams can free themselves from repetitive tasks, gain data-driven insights, and adapt to customer needs in real-time.

This translates to increased productivity, closed deals, and a competitive edge in the dynamic sales landscape.

Remember, adopting AI shouldn't be solely focused on immediate sales figures. By considering the multifaceted benefits, you can create a holistic strategy that fuels long-term success and a happier, more efficient sales team.

How to Leverage AI in Sales?

Let's delve into five key areas where AI empowers your team to achieve unprecedented results:

1. Data Enrichment and Insights: Ditch manual data entry and unlock deeper insights. AI organizes and extracts meaning from disparate sources, enriching your CRM with a holistic understanding of prospects and customers. Tools like HubSpot's predictive scoring utilize AI to identify high-value leads with uncanny accuracy, while Zoho's DataPrep transforms existing information into actionable data points like lead sentiments and topics of interest. Imagine your team armed with such comprehensive intelligence, tailoring strategies, and easily exceeding quotas.

2. Conversation Intelligence: AI-powered conversation intelligence tools transform traditional sales calls into invaluable learning experiences. Platforms like Chorus analyze calls, unearthing key trends, objections, and even competitor mentions. Imagine pinpointing areas for improvement with pinpoint accuracy and coaching your team to close deals with laser focus. AI empowers your sales force to constantly learn, evolve, and dominate the competition.

3. Sales Enablement Automation: Imagine streamlining time-consuming tasks like RFP responses, freeing your team to focus on what they do best: selling. RocketDocs leverages AI to dynamically build proposal content libraries, automatically pulling data for seamless RFP completion. AI-

powered sales enablement solutions encompass intelligence platforms, outreach platforms, and even CRMs, automating tasks and empowering your team to sell smarter, not harder.

4. Pipeline Management and Forecasting: Inaccurate forecasts hamper strategic decision-making. AI solutions like Aviso utilize data analysis to generate reliable WinScores, AI-powered forecasts, and dynamic scenario simulations. With such data-driven insights, your team can build accurate forecasts, make informed decisions, and confidently navigate the pipeline with unparalleled precision.

5. Streamlined and Optimized Engagement: AI doesn't replace the human touch; it amplifies it. By understanding customer needs and pain points (as highlighted by Salesforce's State of Sales report), AI empowers your team to personalize every interaction. Platforms like Apollo leverage AI to automate outreach with pre-defined customization and A/B testing, offering real-time insights into prospect interest. Imagine building meaningful relationships at scale, personalizing communications with laser focus, and converting leads with unprecedented efficiency.

Forging a Sales AI Strategy: 4 Pillars for Success

A well-defined strategy is crucial before diving headfirst into the latest AI fad. Here are four key pillars to guide your journey towards an AI-powered sales revolution:

1. Realistic Goals and Clear Expectations

As with any expedition, knowing your destination is paramount. Clearly defined, achievable, and measurable sales objectives form the bedrock of your AI strategy. Ensure transparency and alignment across your team, communicating both the "what" and the "why" to build buy-in and manage expectations. Remember, Rome wasn't built in a day, so be patient with the adoption process and encourage open communication and learning within your team.

2. Aligning AI with Your Business Landscape

Shiny objects might grab attention, but remember, AI tools should serve your specific needs, not the other way around. With an abundance of options available, carefully evaluate each solution for its potential to contribute to your overall business goals, whether it's accelerating growth, boosting brand awareness, or enhancing customer experience.

3. Targeting Early Victories

Showcase the power of AI by focusing on a project with a short turnaround time (6-12 months). Not only will you demonstrate the tangible benefits to leadership, but you'll also ignite team enthusiasm. Identify high performers in harnessing AI for customer interactions and utilize their experiences as valuable learning resources for the rest of the team.

Implementation Challenges of AI in Organizations

In 2014, Dr. Julio Mayol, Medical Director and Director of Innovation at the Carlos Clinical Hospital in Madrid, Spain, recognized a challenge: while abundant data was available, extracting meaningful insights to improve patient care proved difficult. Seeking a solution, Dr. Mayol consulted with external technology advisors, leading him to consider artificial intelligence (AI). Following this insight, under Dr. Mayol's guidance, the hospital's innovation unit initiated a project to leverage AI. Rather than opting for a generic solution, the team collaborated closely with a technology provider specializing in AI solutions to co-create an innovative application tailored to their specific requirements.

After a year of development, the AI system was ready for field testing. Initial results, six months later, revealed promising outcomes: the diagnostic and patient risk assessment solution significantly reduced the time required for preliminary patient record assessments by half, achieving a remarkable 95% accuracy rate compared to evaluations by eight expert psychiatrists with over 20 years of experience. An unexpected positive outcome of this efficiency boost was the increased availability of medical staff for consultations and patient care, consequently enhancing customer satisfaction.

Another example of AI application in manufacturing can be seen at Siemens. The company has integrated an AI-powered platform known as the Siemens Digital Enterprise Suite to streamline its manufacturing operations.

This platform leverages machine learning algorithms to scrutinize extensive datasets sourced from diverse origins, including sensors, machinery, and other manufacturing apparatus. Through real-time analysis, the platform provides invaluable insights into production processes, pinpointing areas ripe for optimization and enhancement.

Since the deployment of the Siemens Digital Enterprise Suite, notable enhancements in efficiency and productivity have been observed. Siemens has successfully fine-tuned its manufacturing processes, thereby curtailing downtimes and bolstering overall equipment effectiveness.

Moreover, Unilever is a prime example of AI integration in human resources. The company has adopted an AI-driven recruitment platform named HireVue to streamline its hiring procedures and enhance candidate selection.

These successful implementations of AI stand in contrast to numerous reported failures and discrepancies between firms' AI aspirations and execution, highlighting a need for empirical insights into AI implementation projects.

Below, we have discussed the most common issues organizations face during the application of AI in their operations:

Lack of In-House Expertise

Implementing AI often encounters challenges due to the lack of in-house expertise. In 2018, McKinsey & Company conducted a study on the state of artificial intelligence (AI) in companies, highlighting significant barriers to AI adoption. The primary challenges identified included the absence of a coherent AI strategy within organizations and a 43 percent scarcity of talent possessing the requisite skill sets for AI-related tasks. This shortage extends across various AI-related roles, including data scientists, machine learning engineers, and AI researchers. The complexity of AI technologies necessitates specialized knowledge and skills, which many organizations struggle to acquire or retain within their workforce. Consequently, organizations face difficulties in effectively leveraging AI to drive innovation and gain a competitive edge.

Uncertainty About Where to Implement It

Another significant challenge in AI implementation revolves around uncertainty regarding where to apply AI effectively within an organization's operations. According to a survey conducted by Bitkom, nearly 40% of executives cite identifying the right AI use cases as a major hurdle in AI adoption. The diverse range of potential applications for AI across industries and business functions can overwhelm decision-makers, leading to indecision or misallocation of resources. Furthermore, the lack of clarity on the potential impact of AI initiatives on business outcomes adds to the uncertainty. Without a clear strategic roadmap for AI deployment, organizations risk investing in projects that fail to deliver tangible value or align with overarching business objectives.

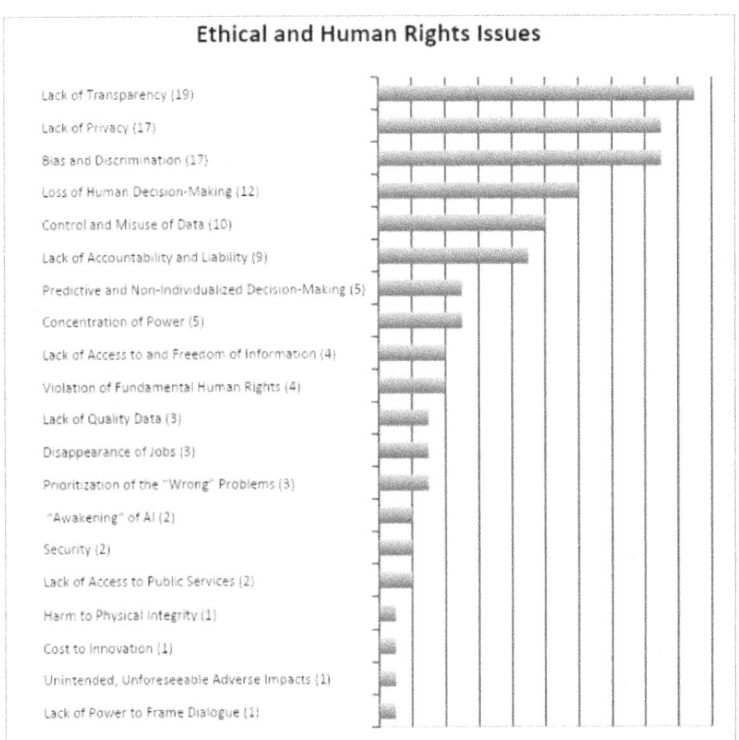

Ethical use of AI

When discussing the ethical considerations surrounding AI, there's often an implicit assumption that we're referring to morally negative aspects. Indeed, much of the AI discourse revolves around addressing morally problematic outcomes. However, it's important to recognize that AI holds the promise of numerous benefits. As highlighted earlier, many AI policy documents emphasize the economic advantages expected to arise from increased efficiency and productivity. These economic benefits translate into ethical values as they promise higher levels of wealth and well-being, ultimately contributing to human flourishing. It's crucial to note that this implies certain levels of wealth distribution and assumptions about the role of society and the state in ethically acceptable wealth redistribution, which should be explicitly addressed.

For instance, the EU's High-Level Expert Group on AI (2019) emphasizes this point, stating that AI is a means to enhance human flourishing, individual and societal well-being, and the common good. Additionally, AI possesses technical capabilities that offer immediate ethical benefits. For example, AI's analytical prowess allows it to process vast amounts of data and identify patterns that humans cannot, leading to deeper insights into various phenomena. This capability can lead to practical improvements in everyday life, such as reducing commuting times or enhancing email spam filters, ultimately making life easier for busy professionals.

Moreover, there's a growing trend of utilizing AI specifically for ethical purposes, often referred to as "AI for Good." However, defining what constitutes ethical goodness is a key challenge in this area. Despite the pluralistic nature of values in society, there have been attempts to identify shared ethical goods or values, such as benevolence, security, achievement, and self-direction. One approach to determining the ethical goods AI should promote is through substantive goods, which are practical outcomes universally accepted to be good. A prominent example of such substantive moral goods is the United Nations' Sustainable Development Goals (SDGs), which represent humanity's consensus on moral aims. The SDGs provide a framework for measuring AI's ethical benefits and are often cited in discussions promoting AI for Good initiatives, such as the UN's AI for Good Global Summit series.

The success of AI is primarily attributed to machine learning techniques, particularly those based on artificial neural networks. However, these approaches raise ethical concerns due to their features, including opacity, unpredictability, and reliance on large datasets for training. The inability of developers, deployers, and users to anticipate system reactions to inputs poses significant ethical dilemmas, especially considering machine learning systems' adaptive and dynamic nature.

Privacy and Data Protection

Privacy and data protection are central ethical concerns in AI, particularly regarding informational privacy. Machine learning's reliance on vast datasets for training raises questions about data protection, with the potential for privacy risks even without direct access to personal data. The emergence of new data types, such as emotional personal data, exacerbates existing challenges, requiring the adaptation of data protection laws to address evolving ethical concerns.

Data Security and Reliability

AI systems introduce new cybersecurity vulnerabilities, including model poisoning attacks, and require novel approaches to vulnerability detection and exploitation. Privacy and data protection issues highlight broader reliability concerns in AI systems, as traditional testing regimes may not adequately assess their performance. The opacity and unpredictability of machine learning systems further complicate reliability assessment, especially in critical domains like healthcare.

According to a survey by Capgemini Research Institute, 69% of organizations believe that they are not fully aware of all AI-related risks, including cybersecurity vulnerabilities. This indicates a widespread concern among businesses regarding the security implications of AI adoption.

Transparency and Accountability

Numerous studies have highlighted instances where machine learning algorithms exhibit biases and perpetuate discrimination. For example, a study conducted by researchers at MIT found that facial recognition systems exhibited higher error rates for darker-skinned individuals, with error rates as much as 34.7% for darker-skinned women compared to 0.8% for lighter-skinned men. Machine learning systems lack transparency, especially in proprietary contexts, hindering accountability and exacerbating issues of bias and discrimination. Lack of transparency makes it challenging to identify and address biases, leading to the reproduction of existing inequalities and human rights infringements. Highlighting the potential for discrimination underscores the importance of transparency and accountability in AI development and deployment.

Justice and Fairness in AI

The use of AI in the criminal justice system and other services raises ethical questions about access to justice and potential biases. Studies have shown that AI applications such as predictive policing may widen existing biases and further marginalize certain population groups. For example, a study by Richardson et al. (2019) found that predictive policing algorithms can disproportionately target minority communities, exacerbating racial disparities in law enforcement. Additionally, the AI Now Institute reports that the reliance on AI in legal processes can broaden existing biases and further disadvantage marginalized populations.

Freedom and Autonomy

AI's influence on individual freedom extends beyond specific applications like parole decisions. According to a study by Lessig (1999), ICT, including AI, can act as a form of law that allows or disallows certain actions, thereby shaping individuals' options for action. Additionally, research by Ryan and Gregory (2019) shows how AI-driven systems, such as traffic management algorithms, can impact individual autonomy by directing actions and choices, sometimes unintentionally. For instance, AI-powered search engines structure users' perceptions and behaviors, potentially limiting autonomy by controlling access to information.

Power Asymmetries and Democratic Principles

AI's economic dominance and structuring of options for action may lead to power asymmetries that jeopardize democratic principles. According to Coeckelbergh (2020), democratic structures may be undermined by the concentration of economic power among tech companies, which utilize user data for profit. Statistics from the scandal involving Facebook and Cambridge Analytica serve as a high-profile reminder of the potential vulnerabilities of democratic processes. Additionally, reports from Isaak and Hanna (2018) highlight concerns about surveillance, manipulation, and threats to democratic values posed by AI technologies.

VR in Business and Sales

Virtual reality (VR) technology provides users with simulated experiences that can mimic or diverge from reality. VR endeavors to immerse users in sensory-rich environments, encompassing visual, tactile, auditory, olfactory, and even gustatory sensations. While its historical roots trace back to the 1800s, VR has evolved significantly, with companies like Oculus, Sony, and Lenovo producing cutting-edge VR products like Oculus Quest and PlayStation VR. In the late 1980s and early 1990s, the US Air Force and NASA Ames initiated VR experiments. Projects like Visually Coupled Airborne Systems Simulator

(VCASS) and Virtual Visual Environment Display (VIVED) aimed to augment pilots' and astronauts' experiences.

Presently, the VR industry is experiencing rapid growth, with the global market expected to expand from under $12 billion in 2022 to over $22 billion by 2025. This growth trajectory encompasses both enterprise and consumer sectors, with particular attention to the burgeoning VR gaming industry, poised to capitalize on the anticipated market expansion.

The potential of VR extends beyond gaming; it's revolutionizing industries such as education, military, medicine, and sports. For instance, Class VR enhances engagement and knowledge retention in education, while Facebook Horizon offers a community-driven VR experience. Moreover, VR enables 360-degree simulations, allowing users to experience anything from historical landmarks to music festivals from the comfort of their homes.

Beyond entertainment, VR finds applications in various other fields. For instance:

Industrial Environments

The proliferation of VR applications in industrial settings has surged following the introduction of Oculus VR's initial headset, alongside the expansion of VR technologies across diverse markets. Companies recognize the benefits of simulating various scenarios in virtual environments, offering advantages over real-world experiences. While practical applications are still limited, numerous concepts and test environments have emerged. One notable application lies in operator and safety training within industrial environments. The objective is to provide employees with training in a risk-free virtual environment before engaging in real-world scenarios. By exposing trainees to unexpected and emergency situations without actual peril, they can acquire valuable experience. This experiential learning enhances memory retention, enabling individuals to better focus on performance-affecting variables when faced with similar situations in the future. Furthermore, companies like Inreal Tech in Germany offer virtual tours of 3D environments, allowing customers to take photorealistic tours through structures before they are physically constructed.

Automobile Industry

The automotive sector is increasingly recognizing the benefits of integrating virtual reality (VR) technology, not only for marketing purposes but also during the design and manufacturing stages. Both Lexus and Volvo have ventured into developing VR simulators to enhance user experiences with their new vehicles.

Lexus has introduced a VR simulator known as RC F Rift, which utilizes an Oculus Rift HMD alongside a real steering wheel and pedals from their Lexus RC F model.

On the other hand, Volvo adopts a different approach, leveraging a mobile phone application in conjunction with Google Cardboard VR during the launch of its XC90 model. By utilizing Google Cardboard, users can insert their mobile devices into a customized cardboard HMD to explore the VR world and experience the XC90 without visiting a Volvo reseller.

Beyond marketing, Audi and Ford are actively incorporating VR into their operations. Audi has developed a VR application for Samsung Gear VR, allowing customers to design personalized cars and visualize both the exterior and interior before making a purchase. Ford, on the other hand, utilizes Oculus Rift internally during the design and development phase to visualize products before physical production. This approach enables them to identify imperfections and implement modifications early in the process, thereby enhancing efficiency and product quality.

Advertising

In the world of advertising, several companies have embraced VR as a marketing strategy to engage with customers. Coca-Cola, for example, utilized VR during the 2014 World Championships in Brazil, allowing people to experience soccer games from the player's perspective through VR HMD devices. Similarly, Thomas Cook offered customers virtual experiences of selected destinations before booking vacations, including virtual helicopter rides over the chosen destinations.

Merrell, an outdoor apparel brand, leveraged VR at the 2015 Sundance Film Festival to rejuvenate its brand and reconnect with core customers. Their "TrailScape" experience allowed users to walk through and experience adventurous hiking trails virtually. Additionally, Inition, a British company, developed a VR experience application for TopShop, offering users front-row seats at London Fashion Shows and live backstage footage.

Notably, all these advertising experiences were designed using Oculus Rift HMD as the primary VR device, highlighting its versatility and effectiveness in creating immersive marketing campaigns.

Virtual Reality (VR) holds significant importance in sales and business for several reasons:

Enhanced Product Visualization: VR enables customers to experience products in a simulated environment, providing a more immersive and realistic representation than traditional photos or videos. This enhanced visualization allows customers to better understand the features, functionalities, and benefits of products, leading to more informed purchasing decisions.

Improved Customer Engagement: VR offers an interactive and engaging way for customers to interact with products, fostering a deeper connection and emotional engagement. By immersing customers in virtual experiences, businesses can capture their attention and hold it for longer periods, increasing the likelihood of making a sale.

In Which Industry Is VR Most Powerful?

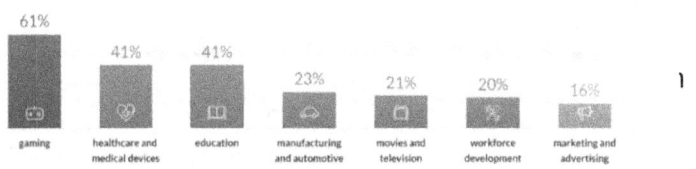

2024: Adoption, Usage & Market Share

Reduced Returns and Increased Conversion Rates: By providing customers with a more accurate representation of products through VR, businesses can reduce the likelihood of returns due to mismatched expectations. Additionally, the sensory nature of VR experiences can lead to higher conversion rates as customers feel more confident and satisfied with their purchases.

Innovative Marketing and Brand Differentiation: Businesses incorporating VR into their sales strategies stand out from competitors and demonstrate a commitment to innovation and technology. VR experiences can serve as powerful marketing tools, attracting attention and generating buzz around products and brands.

Data-driven Insights and Analytics: VR platforms can collect valuable data on customer interactions and preferences, providing businesses with insights into consumer behavior and preferences. This data can inform future product development, marketing strategies, and sales tactics, enabling businesses to make more informed decisions and optimize their operations.

Overall, VR presents a transformative opportunity for businesses to enhance the sales process, drive customer engagement, and differentiate themselves in the marketplace. As the technology continues to evolve and become more accessible, businesses that embrace VR stand to gain a competitive advantage and deliver exceptional experiences to their customers.

Future Tech Trends: Enhancing Customer Engagement

Enhancing customer engagement has become a fundamental aspect of business strategies, with emerging technologies playing a key role in reshaping how businesses interact with their customers. This analysis delves into the transformative potential of Augmented Reality (AR), Internet of Things (IoT), and advanced analytics in revolutionizing the sales process and elevating the overall customer experience.

Augmented Reality (AR): Augmented Reality (AR) technology superimposes digital information onto the physical world, offering immersive and interactive experiences to users. In the realm of customer engagement, AR holds immense promise in transforming the shopping experience. According to Statista, the global AR market is projected to reach $198 billion by 2025, signifying its growing significance in various industries, including retail.

Key Benefits of AR in Customer Engagement:

Enhanced Shopping Experience: AR enables customers to visualize products in real-world settings before making a purchase, thereby reducing uncertainties and increasing confidence in buying decisions.

Personalized Interactions: AR applications can provide personalized recommendations and product demonstrations based on individual preferences and previous interactions.

Increased Customer Satisfaction: By offering engaging and interactive experiences, AR fosters greater customer satisfaction and loyalty, leading to higher retention rates and increased sales.

Example: IKEA Place app allows customers to virtually place furniture in their homes using AR, enabling them to visualize how items would look and fit before making a purchase decision.

Advanced Analytics

Advanced analytics involves the use of sophisticated techniques and algorithms to analyze complex data sets and extract valuable insights. In the context of customer engagement, advanced analytics empowers businesses to understand market trends, predict customer behavior, and optimize marketing strategies.

Key Benefits of Advanced Analytics in Customer Engagement:

Predictive Insights: Advanced analytics models can forecast customer behavior and preferences, enabling businesses to anticipate future trends and tailor their offerings accordingly.

Targeted Marketing: By segmenting customers based on their characteristics and behaviors, advanced analytics enables businesses to deliver personalized marketing messages and offers, resulting in higher conversion rates and ROI.

Continuous Improvement: Through ongoing analysis of customer data, businesses can iteratively refine their products, services, and marketing approaches to better meet evolving customer needs and preferences.

Example: Netflix utilizes advanced analytics to analyze viewer data and recommend personalized content, increasing user engagement and retention.

While virtual and augmented reality are often hailed as the next frontier, there remains a level of uncertainty surrounding their practical applications. Goldman Sachs predicts that the AR/VR industry could reach an annual value of $80 billion by 2025, with $35 billion attributed to software and $45 billion to hardware, showcasing the diverse potential of these technologies.

Like many others, Goldman Sachs researchers view video gaming as the most promising use case for AR/VR technology. Live events and video entertainment are also significant consumer-focused applications.

However, AR/VR's potential extends far beyond consumer applications. Goldman Sachs estimates that nearly half of the industry's revenue will come from the enterprise and public sectors, with healthcare and engineering emerging as particularly promising areas of use.

CONCLUSION

A Vision for Harmonious Prosperity

As the author of this discourse, please reconsider and modify our current business paradigms in the final reflections of this discourse. This suggestion is not only a summation of ideas.

"The company purpose is to create and sell innovative solutions that bring positive value to societal well-being, which in return, will buy your solutions at the right pricing."

Even though it is brief, this statement captures a profound and revolutionary concept that aims to balance commercial innovation with public benefit. It's a scenario in which businesses, particularly those at the cutting edge of technological innovation, combine their entrepreneurial drive with a steadfast dedication to a better society.

The pursuit of profit cannot and should not be separated from the societal circumstances businesses operate in today's increasingly linked and interdependent world. Our discoveries, solutions, and the technology we build must serve a higher purpose than merely maximizing our financial advantage. They ought to demonstrate a desire to support a society that is not just technologically advanced but also defined by sustainability, equality, and well-being.

We must pause and consider what legacy we want to leave behind as we stand on the cusp of historically unparalleled technical developments. The idea establishes a framework in which companies are not only moneymaking machines but also the foundational elements of a functioning society.

In this paradigm, innovation is continuously pursued to enhance social well-being, and each new solution is a step toward a brighter future for everybody.

The adoption of this idea signifies the beginning of an age in which enterprises and society work together for mutual improvement rather than only denoting a shift in commercial methods. In this future, community well-being and personal accomplishment are interconnected routes that lead to a time of peace and prosperity rather than existing in parallel.

In the intricate exploration of the religious and business realms within these pages, it has become evident that the synergy between ethical practices and financial success is not merely coincidental but intrinsically linked. The first part, delving into the depths of spiritual values, emphasizes the significance of integrity and compassion as guiding principles. On the other hand, though structured as a practical guide, the latter section falls short of intertwining these ethical underpinnings into its framework.

However, the overarching theme remains resolute—ethical companies consistently yield higher profits grounded in trust and goodwill. Hence, integrating these values throughout the business narrative is pivotal. By infusing business strategies with the essence of ethical conduct advocated in the first part, businesses can cultivate a culture of trust, fostering long-term partnerships and customer loyalty.

Conclusively, it is imperative to weave the narrative of ethical business practices and religious virtues into a cohesive storyline. By establishing a symbiotic relationship between ethical business operations and financial success, enterprises can ensure profitability and contribute to a more virtuous and prosperous society, aligning with the core principles of our shared faith and promoting a sustainable future built on integrity and compassion.

In light of this, I kindly invite you, eminent readers, leaders in the tech sector, and forerunners of innovation, to embrace this vision, incorporate a dedication to societal well-being into your corporate ethos, and set out on a journey where each step toward innovation is a step toward building a world that thrives in harmony, prosperity, and well-being.

www.ingramcontent.com/pod-product-compliance
Lightning Source LLC
Chambersburg PA
CBHW071054240526
45471CB00015B/1874